DEFINING MOMENTS
THE GREAT DEPRESSION AND THE NEW DEAL

DEFINING MOMENTS
THE GREAT DEPRESSION AND THE NEW DEAL

Kevin Hillstrom

Omnigraphics

P.O. Box 31-1640
Detroit, MI 48231

Omnigraphics, Inc.

Kevin Hillstrom, *Series Editor*
Cherie D. Abbey, *Managing Editor*

Peter E. Ruffner, *Publisher*
Matthew P. Barbour, *Senior Vice President*

Elizabeth Collins, *Research and Permissions Coordinator*
Kevin Hayes, *Operations Manager*

Allison A. Beckett and Mary Butler, *Research Staff*
Shirley Amore, Martha Johns, and Kirk Kauffman, *Administrative Staff*

Copyright (c) 2009 Omnigraphics, Inc.
ISBN 978-0-7808-1049-5

Library of Congress Cataloging-in-Publication Data

Hillstrom, Kevin, 1963-
  The Great Depression and the New Deal / by Kevin Hillstrom.
    p. cm. -- (Defining moments)
  Includes bibliographical references and index.
  Summary: "Explains the history of the Stock Market Crash of 1929 and the Great Depression, as well as President Franklin D. Roosevelt's ambitious program of New Deal reforms. Features include a narrative overview, biographical profiles, primary source documents, chronology, glossary, bibliography, and index"--Provided by publisher.
  ISBN 978-0-7808-1049-5 (hardcover : alk. paper) 1. United States--History--1919-1933. 2. United States--History--1933-1945. 3. Depressions--1929--United States. 4. New Deal, 1933-1939. I. Title.
  E806.H555 2008
  973.91--dc22   2008028658

Printed in the United States

TABLE OF CONTENTS

PRIMARY SOURCES

PREFACE

Throughout the course of America's existence, its people, culture, and institutions have been periodically challenged—and in many cases transformed—by profound historical events. Some of these momentous events, such as women's suffrage, the civil rights movement, and U.S. involvement in World War II, invigorated the nation and strengthened American confidence and capabilities. Others, such as the McCarthy era, the Vietnam War, and Watergate, have prompted troubled assessments and heated debates about the country's core beliefs and character.

Some of these defining moments in American history were years or even decades in the making. The Harlem Renaissance and the New Deal, for example, unfurled over the span of several years, while the American labor movement and the Cold War evolved over the course of decades. Other defining moments, such as the Cuban missile crisis and the terrorist attacks of September 11, 2001, transpired over a matter of days or weeks.

But although significant differences exist among these events in terms of their duration and their place in the timeline of American history, all share the same basic characteristic: they transformed the United States' political, cultural, and social landscape for future generations of Americans.

Taking heed of this fundamental reality, American citizens, schools, and other institutions are increasingly emphasizing the importance of understanding our nation's history. Omnigraphics' *Defining Moments* series was created for the express purpose of meeting this growing appetite for authoritative, useful historical resources. This series will be of enduring value to anyone interested in learning more about America's past—and in understanding how those historical events continue to reverberate in the 21st century.

Each individual volume of *Defining Moments* provides a valuable one-stop resource for readers interested in learning about the most profound events in our nation's history. Each volume is organized into three distinct sections—Narrative Overview, Biographies, and Primary Sources.

- The **Narrative Overview** provides readers with a detailed, factual account of the origins and progression of the "defining moment" being examined. It also explores the event's lasting impact on America's political and cultural landscape.

- The **Biographies** section provides valuable biographical background on leading figures associated with the event in question. Each biography concludes with a list of sources for further information on the profiled individual.

- The **Primary Sources** section collects a wide variety of pertinent primary source materials from the era under discussion, including official documents, papers and resolutions, letters, oral histories, memoirs, editorials, and other important works.

Individually, each of these sections is a rich resource for users. Together, they comprise an authoritative, balanced, and absorbing examination of some of the most significant events in U.S. history.

Other notable features contained within each volume in the series include a glossary of important individuals, places, and terms; a detailed chronology featuring page references to relevant sections of the narrative; an annotated bibliography of sources for further study; an extensive general bibliography that reflects the wide range of historical sources consulted by the author; and a subject index.

Acknowledgements

This series was developed in consultation with a distinguished Advisory Board comprised of public librarians, school librarians, and educators. They evaluated the series as it developed, and their comments and suggestions were invaluable throughout the production process. Any errors in this and other volumes in the series are ours alone. Following is a list of board members who contributed to the *Defining Moments* series:

Gail Beaver, M.A., M.A.L.S.
Adjunct Lecturer, University of Michigan
Ann Arbor, MI

Melissa C. Bergin, L.M.S., NBCT
Library Media Specialist
Niskayuna High School
Niskayuna, NY

Rose Davenport, M.S.L.S., Ed. Specialist
Library Media Specialist
Pershing High School Library
Detroit, MI

Karen Imarisio, A.M.L.S.
Assistant Head of Adult Services
Bloomfield Twp. Public Library
Bloomfield Hills, MI

Nancy Larsen, M.L.S., M.S. Ed.
Library Media Specialist
Clarkston High School
Clarkston, MI

Marilyn Mast, M.I.L.S.
Kingswood Campus Librarian
Cranbrook Kingswood Upper School
Bloomfield Hills, MI

Rosemary Orlando, M.L.I.S.
Library Director
St. Clair Shores Public Library
St. Clair Shores, MI

Comments and Suggestions

We welcome your comments on *Defining Moments: The Great Depression and the New Deal* and suggestions for other events in U.S. history that warrant treatment in the *Defining Moments* series. Correspondence should be addressed to:

Editor, *Defining Moments*
Omnigraphics, Inc.
P.O. Box 31-1640
Detroit, MI 48231
E-mail: editorial@omnigraphics.com

HOW TO USE THIS BOOK

*D*efining Moments: The Great Depression and the New Deal provides users with a detailed and authoritative overview of this event, as well as the principal figures involved in this pivotal episode in U.S. history. The preparation and arrangement of this volume—and all other books in the *Defining Moments* series—reflect an emphasis on providing a thorough and objective account of events that shaped our nation, presented in an easy-to-use reference work.

Defining Moments: The Great Depression and the New Deal is divided into three primary sections. The first of these sections, the **Narrative Overview**, provides a detailed, factual account of the Stock Market Crash of 1929 and the Great Depression, as well as President Franklin D. Roosevelt's ambitious program of New Deal reforms. It explains the economic problems that plunged the nation into the Depression, as well as the impact that this grim era had on millions of American families. This section also explores the ways in which Roosevelt's New Dealers succeeded—and failed—in their efforts to get the country back on the road to prosperity.

The second section, **Biographies**, provides valuable biographical background on leading figures involved in this era, including President Roosevelt and his much-admired First Lady, Eleanor; New Deal official Frances Perkins, who directed Roosevelt's Department of Labor; and Henry Wallace, who became the New Deal's most spirited champion. Each biography concludes with a list of sources for further information on the profiled individual.

The third section, **Primary Sources**, collects essential and illuminating documents from the Great Depression era. This collection includes several of Franklin D. Roosevelt's most famous addresses, excerpts from John Steinbeck's *The Grapes of Wrath*, the Dust Bowl songs of Woody Guthrie, and childhood reminiscences of the darkest days of the Depression.

Other valuable features in *Defining Moments: The Great Depression and the New Deal* include the following:

- Attribution and referencing of primary sources and other quoted material to help guide users to other valuable historical research resources.
- Glossary of Important People, Places, and Terms.
- Detailed Chronology of events with a *see reference* feature. Under this arrangement, events listed in the chronology include a reference to page numbers within the Narrative Overview wherein users can find additional information on the event in question.
- Photographs of the leading figures and major events associated with the Great Depression and the New Deal.
- Sources for Further Study, an annotated list of noteworthy works about the movement.
- Extensive bibliography of works consulted in the creation of this book, including books, periodicals, Internet sites, and videotape materials.
- A Subject Index.

NARRATIVE OVERVIEW

PROLOGUE

On September 15, 1934, a desperate teenager living in Stratford, Connecticut, sat down and wrote a heartfelt letter to a woman named Eleanor Roosevelt. The letter-writer had never met Roosevelt before. But she was inspired to pour out her tale of woe because Roosevelt had a unique status in American life in the 1930s. She was the wife of President Franklin D. Roosevelt, who at that time was fighting to lift the United States out of the most devastating economic depression in the nation's history. Despite his efforts, though, countless American families continued to struggle with the feelings of misery and hopelessness that are so evident in the Stratford teen's anguished letter:

Dear Mrs. Roosevelt,

I am a young girl of only fourteen years, and am writing to you to see if you won't help me, because you helped so many other people. Here is my trouble: My mother has been a cripple since she was five years old. She is a victim of osteomolytis [osteomyelitis, an inflammation of bone marrow] through a Doctor's mistake. These last few years she has been getting worse. She has seven incisions to dress every-day and has had fifteen operations....

I have recently left school to take care of her, while she is home because she has spent the better part of her life in the

---

hospitals. It has cost most of my father's pay every week for medicine and we are up to our neck in hospital bills. I have a younger sister eleven years old who is going to school and must be properly clothed. Now my mother is in the hospital again and is on the danger list. The doctor says this is the end.... We have kept the painful news from our mother because we are afraid it will be too much of a shock. We just pretend we haven't heard from him yet. Dear Mrs. Roosevelt, we all know that within a week or so we won't have our mother anymore and she was so good. Despite all her pains and suffering she still had a cheery disposition. And my dear father has always been so patient giving her everything in his power. We have no money and we know she is going to die. We don't know how we are going to bury her dear body. Please for God's sake help us. Don't let *our mother* be buried in a Potters Field. Please dear Mrs. Roosevelt I implore you help us. *God* will bless you. My daddy doesn't know I am writing this letter. I have written one to President Roosevelt but received no answer. So please help us. You are the only one I can go to now and I know you are kind. Thank You Mrs. Roosevelt and may God bless you.

Tearfully
Miss E.S.

Modern-day readers might find it strange that a girl would turn to the First Lady for help with her family's struggles. But during the Great Depression, Eleanor Roosevelt received thousands and thousands of such letters. She received 300,000 pieces of mail in 1933 alone, and the avalanche of letters from fellow Americans continued throughout the remainder of the decade.

One major reason for the volume of mail that Roosevelt received was her enormous personal popularity. Roosevelt traveled tirelessly all across the United States during the Depression years. Wherever she went, she encouraged poor and struggling Americans, spoke out on social problems like racial discrimination, and publicized the so-called "New Deal" programs that her husband had launched to get the nation back on its feet.

Roosevelt also was a comforting and hopeful voice in newspapers. She regularly published columns and articles that urged Americans to stay strong in spirit and work together to combat the nation's ills. "Mrs. Roosevelt's constant conversation with the public, in which she clearly listened and acted as well as spoke, caused Americans to feel that they did, indeed, know her personally," wrote Cathy Knepper in *Dear Mrs. Roosevelt*. Through the worst days of the Depression, "Eleanor Roosevelt radiated confidence, strength, and, most important of all, hope, serving as a beacon of light in the darkness."[1]

But the other reason that so many people wrote to Roosevelt was that the "darkness" that had overtaken their lives was so complete that it left them with nowhere else to turn. The Great Depression hurled millions of Americans into depths of poverty, fear, and humiliation that they had never experienced before. All across the country, people lost homes, businesses, jobs, life savings, and the ability to provide food, shelter, and clothing for their loved ones.

Some people who suffered economic troubles were shielded from the worst trials of the era by generous family and friends who were not greatly harmed by the Depression. But for many other Americans, their usual sources of help in times of trouble—parents, adult siblings, close friends, business partners—were of no help because they too were trapped in the Depression's web of poverty, hunger, and anxiety. In these cases, life during the Depression became so awful that people were willing to seek out even the most remote possibilities of relief—such as the wife of the president of the United States— to escape the shadow of despair that had fallen over their lives.

Source:
Dear Mrs. Roosevelt: Letters from Children of the Great Depression. Edited by Robert Cohen. Chapel Hill: University of North Carolina Press, 2002, pp. 86-87.

Notes:
1 Knepper, Cathy. *Dear Mrs. Roosevelt: Letters to Eleanor Roosevelt through Depression and War*. Carroll & Graf, 2004, p. xix.

Chapter One

THE ROARING TWENTIES
AND THE GREAT CRASH

⟨━⊶⟨ ∫ ⟩⊷━⟩

The chief business of America is business.

—President Calvin Coolidge, 1924

One of the factors that made the Great Depression so difficult for America to endure was the fact that the years immediately preceding the economic downturn were ones of optimism and prosperity. For much of the 1920s, communities all across the United States experienced exciting levels of economic growth. Good-paying jobs and comfortable homes became realities for greater numbers of American families with each passing year. At the same time, technological developments such as the radio, telephone, and automobile gave Americans more options for entertainment and recreation than ever before. The nation's sense of well-being and affluence became so widespread that the decade became known as "the Roaring Twenties."

But underneath the glitter and laughter of these years, storm clouds of economic uncertainty were gathering. And in the fall of 1929 these clouds let loose a barrage of devastation. Within a matter of weeks, the nation and its people were pulled into the most frightening economic tailspin in the history of the United States.

An Age of Prosperity and Optimism

America entered the 1920s in a mood for peace and stability. The first two decades of the century had been marked by fierce campaigns to reduce political corruption, reduce corporate dominance of American society, extend greater rights to workers, and grant women the right to vote. All of

During the 1920s Americans packed movie houses to watch early film stars such as Joan Crawford, seen here in the 1928 film *Our Dancing Daughters.*

these campaigns received broad public support and enjoyed some success—most obviously in 1920, when the passage of the Nineteenth Amendment gave women the right to vote. But the turmoil that swirled around these efforts had also worn on the American people. The public thirst for domestic tranquility was made even more acute by the horrors of World War I (1914-1918), which resulted in more than 300,000 American casualties, including 116,000 deaths.

America's postwar pursuit of peace and pleasure got off to a roaring start in the early 1920s. Wartime demands had lifted the nation's factories and farms to new heights of production, and when the war ended the economy just kept soaring. One major factor in this continued growth was the steady spread of electricity from city centers to suburbs and even some rural areas. As electricity lit up homes and businesses, manufacturers scrambled to keep up with surging demand for electric-powered hair dryers, radios, refrigerators, phonographs, electric irons, toasters, vacuum cleaners and other consumer products and household appliances. From 1923 to 1929 alone, American manufacturing production jumped by almost 24 percent,[1] and unemployment remained very low.

During this same period, new leisure and entertainment options generated additional economic activity. Movie houses, professional sporting events, and racetracks all enjoyed big popularity booms during the 1920s. In urban areas, nightclubs and jazz halls also exploded in popularity as festive Americans with money in their pockets flocked to downtown destinations to dance, eat, and drink. In these vibrant downtown districts, millions of Americans flouted the nation's anti-alcohol Prohibition laws and caroused late into the night.

Another important factor in America's economic growth during this era was the automobile. The industry was a young one—it did not really burst into being until the opening years of the twentieth century—but the motor car was a revolutionary invention. People loved its practical usefulness as a means to travel to and from the office, the factory, the church, the grocery store, and the neighborhood school. But Americans also loved the symbolism of the automobile. To buyers from coast to coast, the cars produced by legendary automaker Henry Ford and other early manufacturers represented freedom and excitement. As a result, the number of automobiles on American roadways exploded during the 1920s. Manufacturing production tripled over the course of the decade, and more than 5.3 million passenger cars, buses, and trucks were sold across the country in 1929 alone.

The spectacular popularity of the automobile changed American business and society in numerous ways during the 1920s. Railroads and trolley lines withered in the face of this new travel alternative. At the same time, though, the emerging "car culture" spawned a massive variety of restaurants, hotels, gas stations, and other new businesses that catered to automobiles and their owners. "As [the automobile] came, it changed the face of America," wrote journalist Frederick Lewis Allen in 1931. "In thousands of towns, at the beginning of the decade a single traffic officer at the junction of Main

Consumer purchases of automobiles and other expensive products surged during the 1920s after credit purchasing plans came into common usage.

Street and Central Street had been sufficient for the control of traffic. By the end of the decade, what a difference!—red and green lights, blinkers, one-way streets, boulevard stops, stringent and yet more stringent parking ordinances—and still a shining flow of traffic that backed up for blocks along Main Street every Saturday and Sunday afternoon."[2]

Americans were able to purchase large numbers of automobiles—as well as furniture and radios and refrigerators and other consumer products—because their wages were growing steadily. From 1923 to 1929, the average annual earnings of American workers increased by more than 15 percent.[3] But an even bigger factor, especially in the purchase of expensive items like automobiles, was the introduction of credit purchasing plans in the 1920s. Under these plans, Americans had the option of paying for expensive products a little at a time over a period of several months or years, rather than saving up to pay the full purchase price at one time. Installment plans "let millions of Americans have immediately what they might have waited years for in prewar decades," wrote one historian. "Instant gratification in the matter of clothes and gadgets and even automobiles bloated consumer credit from $2.6 billion in 1920 to $7.1 billion in 1929, the largest jump in the country's history."[4]

During these same years, Americans invested in the stock market like never before. In prior decades, the stock market had often seemed like an exclusive club for the wealthy to buy and sell shares in business. But new technology like the telegraph and the telephone made the stock market more accessible to all, and the nation's growing middle class showed great enthusiasm for investing their savings on the New York Stock Exchange and other exchanges around the country. They joined wealthy individuals, banks, and other institutions in snapping up stocks. These purchases gave them small pieces of ownership in a wide range of fast-growing corporations that had been born during the Industrial Revolution. Investing in these companies—U.S. Steel, the Ford Motor Company, General Electric, International Harvester, American Telephone & Telegraph (AT&T), Radio Corporation of America (RCA), and others—came to be seen as an almost sure-fire way of increasing one's personal wealth at little risk. And as the value of these and thousands of other stocks rose, Americans diverted even more of their savings into the market.

The Quiet President

This era of prosperity was overseen by Calvin Coolidge, a quiet, taciturn president who was perhaps most famous for his 1924 declaration that "the chief business of America is business." Coolidge had been elected vice president of the United States in November 1920 on the Republican ticket led by Warren G. Harding. He served quietly in that role for the next two and a half years. During this period, waves of scandal crashed over other areas of the Harding administration, but Coolidge was never implicated in any wrongdoing. On the night of August 2, 1923, Harding suddenly died after suffering a stroke. Coolidge was sworn in as president in the early morning hours of August 3, 1923, and he easily kept the White House in the November 1924 elections.

Calvin Coolidge

President Calvin Coolidge

John Calvin Coolidge was born on July 4, 1872, in Plymouth, Vermont. The son of a storekeeper who also served as a state legislator, Coolidge was a shy and serious youngster. After graduating from Amherst College in 1895 with honors, he became an attorney in Northampton, Massachusetts. He also became active in local Republican politics.

In 1910 Coolidge began a two-year term as mayor of Northampton. He then moved on to become a state senator (1912-15) and lieutenant governor (1916-1918). In the fall of 1918 he eked out a tight victory over Democrat Richard H. Long to claim the governorship of Massachusetts. Two years later, Republican presidential candidate Warren G. Harding selected Coolidge to be his running mate, in large part because of Coolidge's reputation as a staunch pro-business conservative. The Harding-Coolidge ticket triumphed in the fall 1920 election, and in March 1921 Coolidge was sworn in as vice president.

The Harding administration quickly became mired in scandal. The married Harding carried on several affairs, and a number of top officials

Throughout his years in the Oval Office, Coolidge displayed strong pro-business beliefs and showed little interest in tackling social problems. Since the American economy appeared to be thriving, he showed great reluctance to make any policy changes that might slow it down. "Calvin Coolidge honestly believed that by asserting himself as little as possible and by lifting the tax burdens of the rich he was benefiting the whole country—as perhaps he was," explained Allen. "And it was perfectly in keeping with the uninspired and unheroic political temper of the times.... [American business interests] did not want a man of action in the Presidency; they wanted as little governin his administration were implicated in bribery schemes and other forms of public corruption. Coolidge, though, managed to avoid being stained by any of the controversies that swirled around the Harding White House.

On August 2, 1923, Harding died of a stroke while traveling in California. Coolidge was sworn in as the 30th president of the United States in the early morning hours of August 3. Coolidge's top priority upon becoming president was to reassure the country that the Harding era of corruption was over. Over the next five years, the Coolidge administration managed to clean up the reputation of the White House considerably. This was due in no small part to "Silent Cal" himself, who became known far and wide as dull but principled. Coolidge's popularity was also boosted by the roaring 1920s' economy. Some observers charged that Coolidge had little to do with America's prosperity during these years, but others defended him for preserving an environment that was friendly to business.

Coolidge easily won the 1924 presidential election, but in August 1927 he abruptly announced that he did not intend to seek another term. This surprise announcement paved the way for Republican Herbert Hoover to claim the presidency in 1928. After Hoover's inauguration, Coolidge lived quietly in Northampton. He died on January 5, 1933.

Source:
Greenberg, David. *Calvin Coolidge.* New York: Times Books, 2006.

ment as possible, at as low cost as possible, and this dour New Englander who drove the prosperity band-wagon with so slack a rein embodied their idea of supreme statesmanship."[5]

Years later, the legendary journalist H. L. Mencken expressed great relief that Coolidge had not been president when the Great Depression hit America. "In what manner he would have performed himself if the holy angels had shoved the Depression forward a couple of years—this we can only guess, and one man's hazard is as good as another's," said Mencken. "My own is that he would have responded to bad times precisely as he responded to good ones—that is, by pulling down the blinds, stretching his legs upon his desk, and snoozing away the lazy afternoons."[6]

Dark Clouds on America's Horizon

Coolidge's passive approach to governing never changed, even when troubling signs of economic turbulence rippled across the country. Many American farmers, for example, struggled mightily during the 1920s. But their pleas for help were turned aside by the Coolidge administration, despite the fact that about half of the nation's population still relied on agriculture for their livelihood at that time.

The problems in America's farming communities actually had their roots in the years immediately following World War I. For much of the 1910s, American growers of cotton, wheat, corn, and other major crops were able to command good prices for their products because the war had left much of Europe unable to feed itself. Western sheep and cattle ranchers benefited from soaring overseas demand for wool and beef as well. These good times convinced American farmers and ranchers to convert their profits into additional land and machinery. They also borrowed money from banks to expand their operations, and banks were happy to approve these loans because of the high value of farmland.

By the mid-1920s, however, the business environment had completely changed for many farmers. Dairy operators and growers of specialty crops like celery, spinach, and carrots continued to do well, but wheat, corn, and cotton prices all plummeted. These price drops came about because of three main factors: the recovery of European farming operations; increased agricultural output from Canada, Australia, Argentina, and other countries; and heavy American investment in efficient new farming machinery. Together, these three factors created such an oversupply of wheat and cotton that growers could only command a fraction of the price for their goods that they were able to charge a few years earlier. As their earnings declined, farmers found it much more difficult to pay off loans and absorb other operating costs. Bank foreclosures on farms began to rise across America's agricultural heartland. Farmers in Iowa, North Dakota, Minnesota, Kansas, and numerous other agricultural states watched helplessly as their farms plummeted in value. Some farmers and ranchers decided to sell their land at a loss and seek work in the factories of the big cities.

By the late 1920s American farmers and their supporters in Congress were lobbying the Coolidge administration for relief. For example, they urged the government to pass tariffs to increase the price of agricultural commodities imported from foreign growers. But Coolidge and his pro-business allies in Congress flatly refused because of concerns that new tariffs might spark a trade war with Europe that would hurt American manufacturers. Coolidge also vetoed two congressional bills that would have boosted domestic farm prices by establishing a government corporation to buy surplus crops. These decisions made it clear that struggling American farmers were on their own.

Other Warning Signs

American farmers were not the only ones left behind by the general economic prosperity of the 1920s. Textile makers, leather manufacturers, shipbuilders, and other businesses struggled to make ends meet in the postwar years as well. But their struggles went mostly unheard because other industrial factories were churning out greater volumes of goods than ever before.

For a while, American consumer spending kept up with the mountains of automobiles, radios, refrigerators, and toasters that rolled off the nation's assembly lines. By the late 1920s, though, products of all shapes and sizes were sitting on shelves for longer and longer stretches of time. Factories were simply producing more goods than American buyers wanted. Looking back on this period, humorist and social commentator Will Rogers expressed amazement at the situation. "Gosh, wasn't we crazy there for a while?" he wrote in 1932. "Did the thought ever enter our bone head that the time might come when nobody would want all these things we were making?"[7]

"Gosh, wasn't we crazy there for a while?" declared Will Rogers. "Did the thought ever enter our bone head that the time might come when nobody would want all these things we were making?"

The American economy showed other cracks as well. Housing construction slowed through much of the nation in the late 1920s, and banking interests, real estate developers, oil executives, and other speculators roamed feverishly across the country in search of the next big fortune. Their greedy activities triggered economic turmoil in Florida, California, and several other states. But the government made little effort to restrain these activities, even as evidence mounted that the banking industry—the heartbeat of the U.S. economy—was in growing distress.

In 1929 Herbert Hoover succeeded fellow Republican Calvin Coolidge in the White House.

From the end of the Civil War in 1865 until 1920—a stretch of 55 years—a total of 3,100 American banks had shut their doors because of financial problems. But between the end of 1920 and the end of 1929, more than 5,700 banks failed. In 1926 alone, nearly 1,000 banks across the United States failed. Virtually all of these failures stemmed from some combination of poor investments, bad loans, shaky leadership, and inadequate government regulation.

Yet the rising toll of bank failures did not convince Coolidge or the pro-business Congress in Washington to take decisive action. Instead, they simply saw the failed banks as casualties of a keenly competitive business environment. According to their viewpoint, the capitalist system that had been unleashed during the 1920s was bound to leave some people behind, even as it lifted the majority to greater heights of economic power.

Hoover Takes the Reins

On August 2, 1927, Coolidge issued a surprising announcement that he did not intend to run for president in 1928. He offered no explanation for this decision. Some scholars believe that it might have been due to concerns about his health. Other historians speculate that Coolidge knew that an economic downturn was coming and did not want to be in the Oval Office when it arrived.

Whatever his reasons, Coolidge's decision to step aside at the conclusion of his term created a fierce contest for the White House between Democratic nominee Alfred E. Smith and Republican nominee Herbert Hoover (see biography of Hoover, p. 121). Republicans portrayed Hoover—who had been Secretary of Commerce for both Coolidge and Harding—as a leader who would continue the pro-business policies that had brought prosperity to many Americans. In addition, some Republican operatives took advantage of anti-Catholic bigotry to paint Smith, who was Catholic, as someone who would show more allegiance to the Pope than the U.S. Constitution. Both of these strategies were effective. Hoover easily cruised to victory with 58 percent of the popular vote.

Hoover was sworn into office as the 31st president of the United States on March 4, 1929. In his inauguration speech, Hoover expressed great confidence in the nation's future prospects. "Ours is a land rich in resources; stimulating in its glorious beauty; filled with millions of happy homes; blessed with comfort and opportunity," he declared. "In no nation are the fruits of accomplishment more secure. In no nation is the government more worthy of respect. No country is more loved by its people. I have an abiding faith in their capacity, integrity and high purpose. I have no fears for the future of our country. It is bright with hope."[8]

A Grim Warning

Midway through the 1928 presidential campaign, American investors in the stock market received a frightening jolt. On June 12, stocks in numerous industries plunged without warning, causing some unfortunate investors to lose significant sums of money. But the market steadily regained much of the ground it had lost in June through the rest of the summer and the fall. Some individual stocks registered truly spectacular increases in value. A share of stock in RCA, for example, was worth $77 in early March 1928. By New Year's Eve of 1928, though, that share was worth $400. This sort of growth in value reassured most Americans that the stock market remained *the* best place in America to make one's fortune.

> *"Sooner or later a crash is coming, and it may be terrific,"* warned Wall Street veteran Roger Babson. *"The vicious circle will get in full swing, and the result will be a serious business depression."*

The stock market continued to soar through the spring and summer of 1929 as well. On a single day in July, for example, the total value of American Telephone and Telegraph (AT&T) stock increased by more than $75.8 million (at a time when $5 a day was considered good pay). By early September the Dow Jones Industrial Average (DJIA)—a stock market index that tracks the stock performance of leading industrial companies—was five times higher than it had been in 1924.

Yet the euphoria over the stock market's record performance did not fool everyone. In mid-summer 1929 a few Wall Street analysts hesitantly expressed concern that some stocks' prices had become inflated beyond their true value. They worried that if this so-called "bubble" popped and stock prices suddenly plummeted, investors would lose a lot of money. Corporate executives, lawmakers, and other Wall Street boosters loudly dismissed these warnings as whiny pessimism. On September 5, though, a nationally known Wall Street analyst named Roger Babson bluntly told a group of business executives in New York City that "sooner or later a crash is coming, and it may be terrific.... factories will shut down ... men will be thrown out of work ... the vicious circle will get in full swing, and the result will be a serious business depression."[9]

Babson's chilling prediction cut through the irrational optimism on Wall Street. For the next several weeks, brokers and investors alike watched nervously as the stock market veered up and down like a rollercoaster. The uncertain atmosphere caught the attention of other interested parties as well. Some banking institutions decided to rein in their loan operations, and others began to reconsider whether it was wise for them to invest so much of their depositors' money in the stock market. Officials within the Hoover administration, meanwhile, quietly began to debate ways of calming the market. As it turned out, though, the realization that the market was in trouble came far too late.

The Crash Begins

On Monday morning, October 21, 1929, the New York Stock Exchange—the flagship exchange of the U.S. stock market—and every smaller stock exchange in America abruptly began a nightmarish eight-day journey into the depths of despair. From the moment the exchanges opened that morning, brokers showed far more interest in selling stocks than in buying them. They wanted to sell the stocks while their cash value was still high, thus assuring them of a maximum profit. But when they were unable to find buyers, the price of the stocks started to slide until buyers finally began to take orders.

The same phenomenon unfolded the following day. But it was not until Wednesday, October 23 that investors and brokers truly began to understand the fearsome path that they were on. Desperate sellers fought to get rid of their stocks before the market dropped even further, but their actions just triggered an even greater wave of sell-offs. On Wall Street and other exchanges, the volume of traded stock became so great that their ticker tape machines—devices that automatically recorded each transaction that

An anxious crowd gathers outside the New York Stock Exchange during the Great Crash of 1929.

occurred on the exchange floor onto narrow ribbons of paper, or tape—fell hopelessly behind. At the New York Stock Exchange, the tape spewed out its record of stock transactions for 104 minutes after the day's trading finally ended. Investors across the country were in a full-blown panic, desperate to sell their stocks before they became worthless.

On "Black Thursday"—October 24—the nightmare deepened. Stock prices continued to plummet in front of the horrified eyes of people on the exchange floors. Anxious crowds began to gather out on Wall Street in downtown Manhattan. Some of America's leading banking institutions tried to halt the panic by bidding on a number of high-profile stocks. They hoped that when investors saw that they were willing to buy stocks, the investors would follow their example. But the panicked sell-off continued, and when the day's trading finally ended, more than 12.8 million shares had been sold—most of them at prices that were a fraction of their worth only a week earlier.

"Black Tuesday"

The stock market slowed its free fall on Friday and during Saturday's half-day of trading. But as Sunday—the one day of the week in which the exchanges were closed—ticked by, people across the country waited anxiously to see what would happen when the markets re-opened on Monday morning. As feared, the sell-off of stocks continued on Monday. But the worst blow came on "Black Tuesday," October 29.

During that day's trading, more than $10 billion in market value—about $121 billion in 2007 dollars—evaporated. The toll was so great that it remains the single most notorious day in American financial history. "People began to collect under the big brooding statue of Alexander Hamilton in front of the [Stock] Exchange building as word of what was happening on the Exchange floor drifted like rancid wood smoke through downtown New York," wrote one historian. "Soon there were ten thousand people in the narrow street.... Inside the Exchange, brokers stood on the floor gape-mouthed and weeping while the losses mounted in a frenzy of sales that by closing had surpassed 16.4 million shares."[10]

Black Tuesday was the final blow in an eight-day onslaught that brought the world's greatest economic superpower to its knees. The stock market crash destroyed hundreds of corporations across America and blew away the life savings of hundreds of thousands of investors. Men and women who had worked hard their entire lives to build up money for their retirement suddenly found that they had to start all over again. But those who merely lost their retirement stash were among the lucky ones. Countless other investors were completely ruined, left without savings to keep their homes and businesses. Reports of suicide among the legions of Americans who had lost everything to the crash proliferated in the final days of 1929.

The disaster also made America much more vulnerable to the economic problems that had been lurking for much of the decade. Irresponsible banking practices, excessive reliance on credit purchasing plans, overproduction of goods, and the struggles of the farm sector all loomed as much greater threats to the wheezing U.S. economy in the aftermath of the crash. For years, the soaring stock market had masked these "poisons," wrote Allen, but now they spread throughout the nation's economic system. "No matter how many soothsayers of high finance proclaimed that all was well, no matter how earnestly the President set to work to repair the damage with soft words and White House conferences, a major depression was inevitably under way."[11]

Notes:

1 Smiley, Gene. *Rethinking the Great Depression.* Chicago: Ivan R. Dee, 2002, p. 4.

2 Allen, Frederick Lewis. *Only Yesterday: An Informal History of the 1920s.* 1931. New York: Harper Perennial, 2000, p. 142.

3 Smiley, p. 4.

4 Watkins, T.H. *The Hungry Years: A Narrative History of the Great Depression in America.* New York: Owl Books, 2000, p. 8.

5 Allen, p. 160.

6 Quoted in Lathem, Edward Connery, ed., *Meet Calvin Coolidge: The Man Behind the Myth.* Brattleboro, VT: Stephen Green Press, 1960, p. 57.

7 Quoted in Watkins, p. 48.

8 Quoted in Warren, Harris Gaylord. *Herbert Hoover and the Great Depression.* New York: Oxford University Press, 1959, p. 53.

9 Quoted in Galbraith, John Kenneth. *The Great Crash, 1929.* Boston: Houghton Mifflin, 1959, pp. 89-90.

10 Watkins, p. 32.

11 Allen, p. 294.

Chapter Two

THE HOOVER YEARS

The Stock Market Crash of 1929 prompted President Herbert Hoover and other top U.S. officials to take a number of steps to try to return the shell-shocked American economy to health. During this time, Hoover himself repeatedly assured the American people that everything was going to be all right. But waves of terrible financial news continued to wash over the country. In 1930 and 1931, factories and stores all across the nation shuttered their doors, and millions of men and women lost their jobs. Poverty and outright starvation threatened many families, and fear and desperation caused some Americans to turn against one another. A Great Depression had taken hold of the country, and no one knew when—or even if—it would end.

Despite these grim developments, however, Hoover refused to mobilize the power of the federal government against the Great Depression. Holding fast to a conservative political philosophy that opposed federal intervention, he called on local government, church groups, and charitable organizations to help desperate American families weather the storm. When this approach proved completely inadequate to the challenge, the American people turned against Hoover. They elected his opponent, Democrat Franklin D. Roosevelt, in the presidential election of 1932.

An Appeal to Business Leaders

After the horrible stock market meltdown of October 1929, some members of the Hoover administration and conservative Republicans in Congress insisted that the United States did not face a crisis. Treasury Secretary Andrew Mellon even claimed that the economic downturn would benefit the American economic system in the long run. According to this logic, wrote one historian, "the many business bankruptcies would eliminate inefficient producers and open larger markets for efficient ones. Distress sales would get second-rate goods off the shelves and make room for better-quality products. Writing off bad debts would clear the way for fresh starts. Lowering wages would reduce costs, leading to higher profits.... Tough, hard-working, efficient types would survive; ultimately, virtue would be rewarded."[1]

Hoover rejected this advice to simply ride out the economic storm. Instead, he released several reassuring public statements about the fundamental health of the economy and organized a series of meetings with the nation's leading industrialists. Calling on their patriotism and their own self-interest in seeing a return to stability, he asked the executives to continue investing, to avoid massive layoffs, and to maintain wages at current levels. Most of the executives told Hoover that he could count on them. Henry Ford, the most successful automobile maker in the world at the time, even promised the president that he would raise wages from $5 a day to $7 a day.

In the first few weeks of 1930, it appeared that the soothing words and actions of Hoover and America's most prominent businessmen might actually work. The stock market actually registered modest gains in value during the first quarter of 1930, as investors who still had money cautiously looked for bargains. As historian Frederick Lewis Allen wrote in 1931, "it seemed as if perhaps the hopeful prophets at Washington were right and prosperity was coming once more and it would be well to get in on the ground floor and make up those dismal losses of 1929."[2]

Throughout the spring and early summer, the Hoover administration projected an air of confidence about the economy. In March, Julius H. Barnes, who headed the administration's National Business Survey Conference, declared that "the period of grave concern" was over and that "American business is steadily coming back to a normal level of prosperity."[3] In June, Hoover himself dismissed a proposal from a group of ministers and clergymen to establish a federal public works program to help the rising ranks of unemployed. "You have come sixty days too late," he told them. "The depression is over."[4]

The Bottom Falls Out

During the second half of 1930, however, all of the assurances issued by the Hoover administration and corporate spokesmen began to unravel. Companies of all shapes and sizes began to shed workers in a desperate effort to regain profitability. By December 1930 the national unemployment rate hovered around 14 percent—11 percent higher than it had been a year earlier. Prices of products from food to clothing to appliances steadily dropped, but stores continued to have trouble attracting customers.

After the Stock Market Crash of 1929, President Herbert Hoover recruited business leaders to help him reassure the public that the economy was in good health.

In addition, drought conditions across the South ruined economically vital cotton crops and devastated hundreds of rural communities. African-American families, who already endured everyday violence and discrimination in the "Jim Crow" South, were particularly hard-hit because of their extremely limited financial resources. Southern farmers thus joined the impoverished ranks of Midwestern and Great Plains farmers, who found themselves selling their crops for a fraction of what it cost to raise them.

Finally, America's corporate leaders—who had promised Hoover that they would continue pouring money into the economy—abandoned this course of action. Instead, most of them turned to strategies of self-preservation. They stopped investing in new factories, equipment, and transportation. Between the end of 1929 and the end of 1932, gross domestic investment by the private sector declined from $35 billion to $3.9 billion—a drop of almost 87 percent in just three years.[5] At the same time, many of these same corporations started slashing jobs from their payroll. Even Henry Ford pulled away from the promise he had made to Hoover. He did not implement his $7-a-day

The Depression brought a massive wave of evictions of families who could find no way to pay their rent. This Detroit family was evicted from their home in December 1929.

wage until 1931—and he paid for this increase by firing thousands of workers and subcontracting much of the automaker's work to independent companies that paid as little as 12.5 cents an hour.[6]

Hoover responded to these frightening trends by urging each American citizen to "maintain his self-reliance." Turning aside growing calls to provide federal assistance for the hungry and impoverished, he insisted that individual state governments and local communities "should assume [their] full responsibilities for organization of employment and relief of distress." He also called on churches and charities to provide relief to the millions of Americans who were being battered by the recession (see "Herbert Hoover Predicts a Quick Recovery," p. 158).

With great reluctance, Hoover also finally decided to use some of the resources of the federal government to combat the effects of the Depression. The most notable action he took in this area was to sign the Hawley-Smoot Tariff Act of 1930. The idea behind the act was to lift the economic fortunes of American farmers and manufacturers by raising tariffs on goods imported from Europe and other parts of the world. The tariffs, it was thought, would increase prices on foreign goods to a point that American consumers would buy less expensive American-made products. As their sales rose, American businesses would regain profitability, bring fired workers back onto their payrolls, and resume investing in new machinery and other operations.

Instead, the Hawley-Smoot Tariff Act worsened economic conditions in both the United States and Europe. It crushed European farmers and manufacturers, who were also grappling with hard economic times. Within a matter of months, European purchases of American goods plummeted. This development convinced U.S. companies to initiate a new round of layoffs and wage-slashing. Major corporations including Chrysler, Westinghouse, Goodyear,

Firestone, National Cash Register, U.S. Rubber, General Electric, and U.S. Steel all cut wages by 10 to 25 percent in 1931.

Not all of Hoover's decisions were so disastrous. The president approved modest federal programs that put unemployed Americans to work building roads, sewers, and other public works. Hoover also convinced Congress to make small cuts in personal and corporate income taxes as a way to get more spending money in the hands of consumers and business owners. Every step of the way, though, Hoover maintained his staunch opposition to any proposals that would greatly expand the federal government's authority over business practices or its role in social relief efforts. Doing so, he claimed, placed the nation at risk of falling under the spell of "a centralized despotism [that] would destroy not only our American system but with it our progress and freedom."[7]

American Banking in Ruins

Hoover's reluctance to intervene directly in America's escalating banking crisis proved particularly damaging in the early 1930s. The nation's banking system had shown signs of instability throughout the 1920s, a period in which more than 5,700 banks failed. But after the stock market crash of 1929, the entire system teetered on the brink of ruin.

In 1930 more than 1,300 banks across the United States shut their doors. Most of these banks had invested much of the money they received from depositors into the stock market during the 1920s. When the market crashed, the depositors—ordinary Americans from all walks of life—lost millions. The crash also triggered a major "run" on banks. During these runs, depositors rushed to savings institutions to withdraw their money and keep it at home until the economy improved. Since many banks did not have enough money on hand to withstand these runs, they in turn demanded immediate repayments of business loans that they had made to local businesses. But in many cases this desperate strategy not only failed to stave off bankruptcy, it also dragged cash-starved local businesses down with the banks. A bank failure, then, was a devastating event in any community—and especially in rural areas where a single bank often served an entire town and the surrounding population.

Banks continued to close by the hundreds in 1931. In the fall of that year Hoover responded by calling a meeting with the nation's leading bank execu-

By the end of 1930, employment agencies in cities and towns across the country were being swamped by desperate men and women seeking work.

tives. The president gave the bankers $500 million to form the National Credit Corporation (NCC). This entity, which was to be managed by the bankers, was given a mandate to distribute the $500 million in federal funds to banks that they thought could survive with a little help. But the NCC leadership proved so reluctant to risk any of the funds that the effort withered and died within a year.

In 1932 Hoover tried another tactic. Working with Congress, he created the Reconstruction Finance Corporation (RFC) to lend federal funds to troubled banks, railroads, insurance companies, and local governments. Lawmakers also passed measures to give federal reserve banks more flexibility to make loans to struggling banks. These initiatives helped many banks to stay solvent. But these steps were too modest and came far too late to halt the general downward slide. By the time Hoover's presidency ended in March 1933, America's banking system had become paralyzed. Over $140 billion in savings had been lost to bank failures, and the banks that survived the slaughter were very reluctant to make loans of any kind to individuals or businesses. Across much of America, checks could not even be used to pay for the simplest items because no one knew whether the checks were worthless or not.

Desperate Times

As the flow of money through the American economy slowed to a trickle, tens of thousands of businesses collapsed. Wages in manufacturing industries plunged from $16 billion in 1929 to less than $7.7 billion in 1932. The U.S. Gross National Product (GNP), the total dollar value of all goods and services produced for consumption during a given period of time, slumped from $104 billion in 1929 to $41 billion in 1933.[8] By 1933, nearly 150,000 farms were being lost to foreclosure every year.

During these grim months, conditions in many parts of America deteriorated with startling speed. Fully half of the workers in Detroit, the automotive capital of the world, were without jobs by the end of 1930. Cities like Chicago, Boston, and Philadelphia struggled with unemployment rates that hovered between 30 and 40 percent. By September 1932, the national unemployment rate was a shocking 28 percent.[9]

Food riots broke out in many parts of the country. Desperately hungry people pillaged grocery stores and food storehouses in Minneapolis, San Francisco, Oklahoma City, St. Louis, and many smaller communities in the early 1930s. Unemployment marches organized by unions and left-wing

Rising levels of poverty and desperation sparked hunger marches in many parts of the nation, including this one in Pontiac, Michigan.

political groups also sprouted in cities from coast to coast, and on several occasions these marches ended in violent clashes with police officers or national guard troops. In March 1932, for example, a march of unemployed auto workers on a Ford plant in Dearborn, Michigan, erupted into a clash with police that left four marchers dead and sixty wounded. Henry Ford's fear of revenge attacks became so great after this that he installed machine-gun nests around his Dearborn estate.[10]

Many cities used up so much of their limited funds on relief efforts for the poor that they had to fire vital personnel like firemen, policemen, and teachers. In these same cities, homeless individuals and families—many of whom had lived in comfortable middle-class surroundings only a year or two earlier—gathered in clusters of tin and cardboard shacks. They called their makeshift villages Hoovervilles in bitter tribute to the president, whom they saw as both incompetent and uncaring.

The disillusionment of Hooverville residents was shared by millions of other Americans. Even those who were not reduced to homelessness or daily pangs of hunger still felt betrayed by the onset of the Great Depression. "The kind of readjustment they are called upon to make is heroic," Episcopal Bishop John Paul Jones observed in the pages of *Survey Graphic* in 1933. "Vast multitudes of them have lost financial security forever. In bewilderment and bitterness they will seek a sign of hope, and no sign will be given. Some will give up and end it all, but a great majority will go on living some kind of broken and frustrated lives."[11]

The hard times also heightened tensions between different ethnic groups. Discrimination and violence against immigrants and African Americans surged in many parts of the country, as native-born whites scrambled to keep the dwindling numbers of jobs for themselves. All across the Deep South—and in many parts of the North—signs were posted bluntly telling African Americans not to bother applying for a job until every white man was employed. Under pressure from working-class whites, Hoover also took steps in 1930 to halt most legal immigration into the United States. The administration's steps were extremely effective. In the first five months of 1931 alone, nearly 100,000 aliens who normally would have received visas were refused entrance into the country because of these changes. Advocates for immigrants protested, but to no avail.

Stories of Despair

As the Depression deepened, sad scenes of misery and despair were everywhere (see "Remembering a Depression Childhood," p. 155). Theatre producer Herman Shumlin recalled that when walking through New York City's Times Square,

> You'd see these men, silent, shuffling along in line. Getting this handout of coffee and doughnuts.... [They wore] shabby clothes, but you could see they had been pretty good clothes. Their faces, I'd stand and watch their faces, and I'd see that flat, opaque, expressionless look which spelled, for me, human disaster. On every corner, there'd be a man selling apples. Men

31

A Worldwide Depression

Nazi leader Adolf Hitler in 1933.

The United States was not the only nation that suffered a severe economic downturn in the 1930s. In fact, the Great Depression was a worldwide phenomenon. Industrialized countries in Europe and elsewhere experienced the same crushing combination of unemployment, poverty, factory closures, and farming foreclosures that afflicted the United States. The collapse of international trade with the United States and other major trading partners further added to the financial problems of all countries.

Cities and regions that were heavily dependent on manufacturing, mining, and agriculture suffered the most, but no area escaped unscathed. And in some countries, conditions became so bad that they triggered political instability and chaos. In Germany, for example, public anger, resentment, and hopelessness about poor economic conditions contributed to the emergence of Adolf Hitler and the Nazi Party in the 1930s.

in the theater, whom I'd known, who had responsible positions. Who had lost their jobs, lost their homes, lost their families. And worse than anything else, lost belief in themselves. They were destroyed men.[12]

Chicago social worker Louise Armstrong recalled that the people who lived through the Depression "saw the city at its worst…. One vivid, gruesome moment of those dark days we shall never forget. We saw a crowd of some fifty men fighting over a barrel of garbage that had been set outside the back door of a restaurant. American citizens fighting for scraps of food like animals!"[13]

People in rural areas reported similar tales of anguish. From the coal mining towns of the Appalachians to the timber, ranching, and farming communities of the West, stories of starving children, desperate thievery, and men and women who gave themselves up to alcohol to blot out the pain of the Depression spread like wildfire. Foreclosures soared on ranches, farms, and businesses that depended on ranchers and farmers for their livelihoods.

Ranchers and farmers that managed to keep their land, meanwhile, expressed fury and helplessness at the measures they had to take to survive. One Oklahoma City newspaper editor recalled a 1931 conversation with a Western sheep rancher. "He said that he had killed 3,000 sheep this fall and thrown them down the canyon, because it cost $1.10 to ship a sheep, and then he would get less than $1 for it. He said he could not afford to feed the sheep, and he would not let them starve, so he just cut their throats and threw them down the canyon."[14]

In California, meanwhile, incredible volumes of produce rotted on lots and in warehouses because growers could not find buyers—and because they were unwilling to give their crops away. "In 1932 in Imperial Valley alone, 1.4 million crates of cantaloupes, 2.8 million watermelons, and 700,000 lugs of tomatoes [were] destroyed," wrote one historian. "In the orange groves that stretched nearly unbroken for more than seventy miles from Arcadia to beyond Riverside, hundreds of tons of unsold oranges a week were piled up in huge mounds, covered in thick heating oil to discourage pilfering, and left to rot in the full view of those who could have used them."[15]

> *"Vast multitudes of [Americans] have lost financial security forever," mourned one Episcopal Bishop. "In bewilderment and bitterness they will seek a sign of hope, and no sign will be given. Some will give up and end it all, but a great majority will go on living some kind of broken and frustrated lives."*

Valiant but Doomed Relief Efforts

As reports of food riots, angry mobs of unemployed workers, and penniless families proliferated, state, county, and city officials frantically called for federal assistance. "I cannot believe that a national government will stand by while its citizens freeze and starve, without lifting a hand to help," said Pennsylvania Governor Gifford Pinchot in January 1932. "I do not see how it can refuse to grant that relief which it is in honor, in duty, and in its own interest bound to supply."[16] But Hoover clung to his conservative principles and would not budge.

Hoover's decision to keep the federal government from shouldering any of the burden for relief efforts placed enormous pressure on individuals, charitable groups, religious organizations, and state and municipal governments across the nation. Some groups and agencies mounted valiant crusades against the poverty and hopelessness that stalked their communities during the early years of the Depression. Others were less willing or able to help. Several surveys of the period, for example, indicated that wealthy Americans were far less generous in donating to charities during the Depression than working-class people who were actually much more vulnerable.

Among state governments, only eight states ever set aside significant amounts of money for relief programs for their citizens. The two most effective state relief programs were established in Illinois, under Governor Henry Horner, and New York, under Governor Franklin D. Roosevelt (in 1933, in fact, Roosevelt made extensive use of the New York model of relief when he took over as president and launched his New Deal programs).

At the local level, many cities and counties were overwhelmed by the task of caring for the hungry and homeless. Thousands of cities and counties had to slash basic services in education, law enforcement, sanitation, and other areas to pay for relief efforts—and still the plight of citizens worsened.

Some religious and charitable organizations tried to fill this void. Their attitude was aptly symbolized by the words of a New York City rabbi to his synagogue in the early 1930s. "Fifty thousand children are in need of feeding [in the city]," he declared. "What are the synagogues going to do about it? We cannot keep them alive on prayer. We must give them bread."[17] Overall, mainstream Protestant, Catholic, and Jewish congregations did the most to help the poor and hungry during these difficult years. Fundamentalist congregations, on the other hand, were less generous. They tended to interpret the Great Depression as a sign of God's anger and unhappiness with a sinful America.

Other ambitious and generous relief efforts were carried out by the ministries of controversial figures like Reverend Major Jealous Divine in Baltimore and Aimee Semple McPherson in Los Angeles. For many desperate

Americans, the radical politics and untraditional religious beliefs of figures like Divine and McPherson mattered far less than their willingness to provide them with good food and warm shelter. Still, these relief efforts amounted to little more than "bucket brigades fighting a skyscraper fire," wrote Gilbert Seldes in 1933.[18]

The Self-Help Movement

Millions of Americans who accepted charity from their neighborhood church or relief payments from local agencies during the Great Depression did so with the greatest reluctance. These were proud and independent-minded people who had been taught from an early age that hard work and self-reliance were prized attributes. It caused great injury to their self-esteem when they were forced to stand in bread lines to get food for their hungry children, or to go on the "dole"—a term for accepting relief or welfare payments from the government—to obtain the barest necessities of life for themselves and their families.

During the early 1930s, scrappy citizens in many cities formed ambitious "self-help" organizations to minimize their reliance on such assistance. These groups—which called themselves leagues, councils, and associations—put together barter and exchange systems for their members. As many as a million Americans joined these groups in Dayton, Ohio; Omaha, Nebraska; and dozens of other cities of varying sizes.

The most successful of all these groups was Seattle's Unemployed Citizens' League (UCL), which reached a peak of 50,000 members in the early 1930s. UCL members shared tons of garden produce, thousands of cords of firewood, and an estimated 120,000 pounds of fish from the waters of Puget Sound among themselves. By 1932 the organization had proven itself so clever and talented that city officials placed Seattle's entire relief program under the direction of the UCL.[19]

In addition to the self-help movement, countless other Americans helped each other by simply practicing the timeless virtues of compassion and neighborliness. In many parts of the country, stories abounded of people who managed to scrape through the depths of the Depression with the understated but vital help of family, friends, and neighbors. For some, these gestures of human kindness were all that kept them from being swept away in the dark and turbulent waters of the era.

Washington, D.C., policemen carry a protesting World War I veteran off to jail during the 1932 Bonus March riots.

Hoover Raises Taxes

By 1932 the Great Depression was having a measurable impact on the federal treasury. Since individuals and corporations across the country were earning less money, they were also paying less in taxes. Hoover strongly believed that the federal government should avoid operating at a deficit—spending more than it was taking in—at all costs because it would be bad for the economy in the long run. With this in mind, the president convinced Congress to pass a massive increase in taxes so that the federal budget could be balanced. The United States thus imposed major new tax increases at a time when huge numbers of Americans were desperately searching for enough money to keep their homes and feed their families.

The Revenue Act of 1932 doubled normal federal income tax rates for individuals. It also imposed a host of new taxes on the sale of all sorts of goods that were a part of everyday life, from gasoline, tires, and toiletries to electricity and telephone service. This new law infuriated millions of Americans who were already struggling to scratch together enough money to provide basic necessities for themselves and their families. Hoover and his fellow Republicans in Congress, who had been essential in securing passage of the Revenue Act, were vilified from coast to coast.

Hoover's reputation with the American people suffered another big blow in the summer of 1932. In May, an estimated 15-20,000 World War I veterans staged a march into Washington, D.C. to demand immediate payment of cash bonuses for military service that were not scheduled to be distributed until 1945. This Bonus March, as it came to be widely known, attracted nationwide attention. When Congress refused their demand, thousands of veterans set up makeshift camps in the heart of the city and continued with demonstrations. The protests continued as the summer wore on, but some of the camps became public health hazards and dens of lawlessness.

Hoover made several attempts to defuse the stand-off in the early summer, but all of them failed. In July he finally authorized federal troops armed with cavalry and tanks to break up the camps and remove the protestors. On July 28, troops under the command of General Douglas MacArthur (who would later become a famous World War II hero) swarmed into the camps, attacking the homeless veterans with bayonets and tear gas and burning their camps to the ground.

37

In 1932 popular New York Governor Franklin D. Roosevelt defeated Herbert Hoover to claim the White House for the Democratic Party.

The shocked and dispirited veterans fled the capital, and Hoover tried to frame the clash as a triumph for law and order. But most Americans did not agree. As they scanned newspapers plastered with photographs of burning camps and frightened veterans, they raged at the heartlessness of Hoover and the federal government. The treatment of the Bonus Marchers convinced many people once and for all that the Hoover administration simply did not care about the millions of Americans trapped in the Depression's grip.

The Election of 1932

As Hoover prepared for the 1932 presidential elections, the Democratic Party nominated a formidable opponent—New York Governor Franklin D. Roosevelt (see Roosevelt biography, p. 142). During his time as governor, Roosevelt had built a record of support for labor unions, working people, and education. He had also battled the forces of the Depression with great energy. He had provided tax relief for farmers, lobbied for guaranteed pensions for elderly citizens, and created a state relief agency known as the Temporary Emergency Relief Administration (TERA). Under this innovative program, Roosevelt guaranteed cities across the state that for every three dollars they spent on welfare and unemployment programs, the state would give them two dollars for those programs.

Roosevelt's reform record and his popularity with New York voters made him an early frontrunner for the Democratic nomination. Other candidates put up a spirited fight, but in July 1932 he clinched the nomination. Roosevelt flew to the Democratic Convention in Chicago to accept the nomination in person. While in Chicago, he delivered a rousing speech in which he promised "a new deal for the American people."

The battle for the White House between the Republican incumbent and the Democratic challenger turned out to be a rout. The majority of Americans disapproved of Hoover's performance and wanted a change, and they turned out at polling centers in big numbers. When the votes from the November 1932 presidential election were tallied, Roosevelt had received 22.8 million votes—7 million more than Hoover received. In addition, Roosevelt's Democratic Party made huge gains in both houses of Congress. When Roosevelt was inaugurated in March 1933, the Democrats would hold a 313 to 117 advantage over the Republicans in the House of Representatives and a 59 to 36 edge in the Senate. These majorities would make it much easier for Roosevelt to implement his promised "new deal" programs.

In the five-month period between Roosevelt's election and his inauguration, though, the economic state of the nation continued to worsen. Bank failures reached such epidemic proportions that more than 30 states imposed restrictions on bank withdrawals or declared outright "bank holidays"—temporary closures of banks across the state. The nation's two most important banking systems were located in New York City and Chicago. Hoover knew that if the governors of New York and Illinois shut these banks down, the dazed and dispirited American public might descend into full-blown panic. With this in mind, he spent much of his last few days in the White House urging the governors to keep them open. But his efforts failed. On March 4, 1933—Roosevelt's inauguration day—the banks in Chicago and New York were closed, sending ripples of fear and apprehension across the country.

This last defeat seemed to take an especially heavy toll on Hoover. As he handed the reins of government of the United States over to Roosevelt on March 4, Hoover reportedly declared that "we have done all that we can do.... There is nothing more to be done."[20]

Notes:

1 Garraty, John. *The Great Depression.* New York: Doubleday, 1987, p. 32.
2 Allen, Frederick Lewis. *Only Yesterday: An Informal History of the 1920s.* 1931. New York: Harper Perennial, 2000, p. 296
3 Quoted in Allen, p. 296.
4 Quoted in Garraty, p. 32.
5 Chandler, Lester V. *America's Greatest Depression.* New York: Harper & Row, 1970, pp. 21-22.
6 Watkins, T.H. *The Hungry Years: A Narrative History of the Great Depression in America.* New York: Owl Books, 2000, pp. 40-41.
7 Quoted in Garraty, p. 34.
8 *Historical Statistics of the United States, Colonial Times to 1970.* 2 vols. Washington, DC: U.S. Department of Commerce, Bureau of the Census, 1975.
9 Smiley, Gene. *Rethinking the Great Depression.* Chicago: Ivan R. Dee, 2002, p. 21.
10 Smiley, p. 23.
11 Quoted in Watkins, p. 54.

[12] Quoted in Turkel, Studs. *Hard Times: An Oral History of the Great Depression.* New York: Pantheon, 1971.

[13] Armstrong, Louise. *We Too Are the People.* Manchester, NH: Ayer, 1971, p. 10.

[14] Quoted in Bailey, Thomas A., and David Kennedy, eds. *The American Spirit.* Lexington, MA: DC Heath, 1984, vol. 2, p. 739.

[15] Watkins, p. 97.

[16] Pinchot, Gifford. "The Case for Federal Relief," *The Survey,* January 1, 1932.

[17] Quoted in Seldes, Gilbert. *The Years of the Locust (1929-1932).* Boston: Little, Brown, 1933, p. 297.

[18] Seldes, p. 162.

[19] Watkins, p. 96.

[20] Egan, Timothy. *The Worst Hard Time.* Boston: Houghton Mifflin, 2006, p. 132.

Chapter Three

ROOSEVELT AND THE FIRST NEW DEAL

⊸⊸⊸⋘∪∩⋙⊸⊸⊸

The people aren't sure … just where they are going, but anywhere seems better than where they have been. In the
homes, on the streets, in the offices, there is a feeling of
hope reborn.

—Editorial in *Sales Management,* March 15, 1933

After Franklin D. Roosevelt became president in March 1933, he guided a flurry of major new Depression-fighting laws and policies through Congress. Many of these policies and programs were implemented during his first one hundred days in office, and they addressed a wide range of problems facing the American people. Some of them addressed the ailing infrastructure of the economy, while others tackled unemployment, hunger, and the plight of American farmers. Some of these efforts were more success-ful than others. But taken together, they convinced the majority of Americans that the nation was finally moving in the right direction again.

A Daunting Challenge

The challenge that awaited Roosevelt when he entered the Oval Office was enormous. Emotionally, America was still in a state of shock about its meteoric fall from the prosperity of the Roaring Twenties. The nation's economy, meanwhile, had been shattered by the events of the previous three years. By March 1933, unemployment was hovering at 28 percent—and in some major cities unemployment hovered at 40 percent or more. National production of durable manufactured goods such as automobiles, trucks, farm machinery, tires, large household appliances, and business

When Franklin D. Roosevelt (center) became president in 1933, the entire country seemed to take courage from his confident and upbeat attitude.

equipment had plummeted 77 percent from July 1929 to March 1933. Investment in new housing construction had fallen more than 90 percent from 1925 to 1933. And between 1929 and 1933, 10,000 banks across the country had failed.[1]

Despite all this bad news, Roosevelt swept into the White House projecting an image of confidence and enthusiasm for the task ahead. In his inaugural address, he proclaimed that "this great Nation will endure as it has endured, will revive and will prosper" and assured the public that "the only thing we have to fear is fear itself."[2] (see "Franklin D. Roosevelt's First Inaugural Address," p. 162).

These words—and similar declarations that Roosevelt issued over subsequent weeks—seemed to resonate with the American public in a way that Hoover's statements never did. "Roosevelt came in, and that was a cheery moment," recalled Broadway composer Alec Wilder. "Everybody seemed to know it.... His miraculous quality seemed to hit everybody."[3] One week after the inauguration ceremony, the influential journalist Walter Lippmann wrote that "the nation, which had lost confidence in everything and everybody, has regained confidence in the government and in itself."[4] And a mere 15 days after Roosevelt was sworn in as president, journalist Anne O'Hare McCormick wrote in the *New York Times* that "once more there is a government. The capital is experiencing more government in less time than it has ever known before. Always a chameleon city, changing its color with every President, it is now as tense, excited, sleepless and driven as a little while ago it was heavy and inactive."[5]

Ending the Banking Crisis

The renewed sense of hope that Americans felt was in large measure a reaction to Roosevelt's swift and decisive response to the nation's banking crisis. As soon as Roosevelt took office, he called a bank holiday from March 6 to March 9. This holiday gave the administration time to begin a complete review of the fiscal health of every bank in America. Roosevelt then called Congress into session and introduced the Emergency Banking Relief Act, which contained many wide-reaching reforms of the banking system. Members of Congress had virtually no opportunity to read the bill for themselves, but they were so eager to support Roosevelt that they passed it after only forty minutes of debate. Roosevelt signed the bill into law a mere eight hours after it had been introduced in Congress.

The Emergency Banking Relief Act was one of the most important pieces of legislation of the entire New Deal era. It gave the president broad new authority to set credit policies, control currency and gold movements and exchanges, and determine which banks under review would be reopened and which would be liquidated.

Once the act was passed, Roosevelt launched a campaign to enlist public support for it. On the evening of March 12, 1933, he delivered a national radio address on the subject to millions of anxious listeners. During this address, he discussed how his bank rescue plan was going to work. He also urged the American people to support the effort. "I do not promise you that every bank will be reopened or that individual losses will not be suffered, but there will be no losses that possibly could have been avoided; and there would have been more and greater losses had we continued to drift," he said. "Confidence and courage are the essentials in our plan. You must have faith; you must not be stampeded by rumors. We have provided the machinery to restore our financial system; it is up to you support and make it work. Together we cannot fail."

This radio address was the first of Roosevelt's so-called "fireside chats" to the American people. These addresses—so named because many American families of that era sat by their fireplace to listen to the radio—became a hall-mark of the Roosevelt presidency. His fireside chat on the banking crisis was a huge success, for it both informed and reassured the American public. "No president had ever gone to so much trouble to explain to the public in simple language just what was happening and what he and his people were doing," observed one historian.[6]

"Confidence and courage are the essentials in our plan," declared Roosevelt. "You must have faith; you must not be stampeded by rumors. We have provided the machinery to restore our financial system; it is up to you support and make it work. Together we cannot fail."

In June the Banking Act of 1933 (also known as the Glass-Steagall Act) further built on the March legislation. This law created the Federal Deposit Insurance Corporation (FDIC), which guaranteed people who put money in savings accounts that if their bank failed, the federal government would reimburse them for their losses. It also made it illegal for commercial banks to invest depositors' money in the stock market. This latter measure ensured that banks could no longer place the money entrusted to them by depositors at risk by investing it in stocks.

After the passage of these laws, more than 1,100 banks across the United States were dissolved because they were in such awful financial shape. Another 3,000 banks were completely reorganized. But measures taken by the federal government dramatically reduced the pain of these closures and reorganizations to individuals and businesses. And the review process, combined with Roosevelt's salesmanship, convinced the American public that the banks could once again be used safely. By the end of 1933, deposits were once again exceeding withdrawals in the U.S. banking system. In 1936, not one single bank in the United States failed.

The First Hundred Days

Roosevelt's reforms of the banking industry were only the initial steps in what came to be known as "The First Hundred Days." This three-month frenzy of bold legislation reflected the determination of the president and his fellow "New Dealers" to move the country in a dramatic new direction. Some of the legislation that passed during this period—and throughout the New Deal—created short-term programs for the immediate relief of the swelling ranks of hungry, homeless, and unemployed Americans. Other legislation was designed to restore the long-term health of the economy. And some measures—like the Banking Act of 1933—were guided by a desire to fundamentally reform aspects of U.S. business and society.

Roosevelt was by no means the only U.S. politician who created the New Deal slate of programs and policies. Influential U.S. senators like Robert F. Wagner of New York, New Deal administrators such as Harry L. Hopkins and Hugh S. Johnson, and trusted cabinet officials like Harold Ickes (Secretary of Interior), Frances Perkins (Secretary of Labor), and Henry Wallace (Secretary of Agriculture) all played important roles in developing administration policies during the 1930s. Roosevelt also regularly consulted with a New Deal "brain trust"—Columbia University professors Raymond Moley, Rexford Tugwell, and Adolf A. Berle—on important policy matters. The New Deal, summarized one historian, "bore the stamp of many authors, arose from no master plan, and did not fit neatly into a single ideological box."[7]

All of these men and women recognized that the situation across America had become so bad that the president was willing to consider all sorts of ideas. They also recognized that the Democratic-controlled Congress was in a mood to approve just about any request that the president made. With these factors in mind, Roosevelt's inner circle proposed bold policy strokes that never would have had a prayer of serious consideration in more prosperous times.

A Lifeline for American Farmers

After addressing the banking crisis, Roosevelt and his New Dealers next turned their attention to the devastated farming sector. The situation they faced was grim. "Farmers were being run off the land, penniless, while the cities couldn't feed themselves," noted one historian. "The average farmer was earning three hundred dollars a year—an 80 percent drop in income from a decade earlier."[8]

The Tennessee Valley Authority

One of the most ambitious Depression-fighting efforts of Franklin D. Roosevelt's first term as president was the 1933 creation of the Tennessee Valley Authority (TVA). The Tennessee Valley region of the country—which covered a broad swath of seven Southern states—had been particularly hard-hit by the Depression. It had virtually no industry, so the regional population was heavily dependent on agriculture. But much of the land had been farmed too hard for too long, eroding and depleting the soil. Rivers and forests had also suffered at the hands of poor farmers desperate to squeeze every last drop of money out of the land. Only a tiny percentage of farming families had electricity.

A TVA worker operates a jackhammer at a dam site.

After weighing all these problems, Roosevelt and his advisors decided that the region needed special help. The president subsequently asked Congress to create "a corporation clothed with the power of government but possessed of the flexibility and initiative of a private enter-

The legislation that the Roosevelt administration put together—the 1933 Agricultural Adjustment Act (AAA)—was explicitly focused on ending the overproduction that had created such low prices across the country for wheat, hogs, corn, tobacco, cotton, rice, and milk. Under the AAA's crop reduction program, the federal government began paying farmers to keep some fields uncultivated or to otherwise limit production. During this same period, the government bought some surplus food crops and passed them out to the needy. Federal officials even supervised the slaughter of six million surplus pigs and distributed the meat to relief organizations.

As he had done with his banking legislation, Roosevelt used a fireside chat to rally public support for the AAA. "The purchasing power of nearly

prise." On May 18, 1933, Congress obliged by passing the Tennessee Valley Authority Act.

The TVA transformed the entire region within the space of a few years. It harnessed the floodwaters of the Tennessee River and its major tributaries for conversion to electricity. This electricity lit up rural homes for the first time, making life easier and farms more productive. From 1933 to 1945, the number of valley farms that were electrified jumped from 2 percent to 75 percent. Electricity also drew factories and mills into the valley, where they provided much-needed jobs. By the early 1950s, in fact, the TVA was the biggest electric utility in the entire country.

The TVA's impact went well beyond flood control and electricity generation, however. It also taught farmers soil conservation practices that enabled them to improve crop yields, and it helped residents replant forests and manufacture fertilizers. Villages, towns, and cities were all rejuvenated by the economic activity that swirled around TVA projects, and the TVA became the foundation for a half-century of economic development in the South. The TVA remains the primary electricity provider in the Tennessee Valley region.

Source:
Tennessee Valley Authority, "From the New Deal to a New Century." Available online at http://www.tva.gov/abouttva/history.htm.

half our population depends on adequate prices for farm products," he said. "We have been producing more of some crops than we consume or can sell in a depressed world market. The cure is not to produce so much. Without our help the farmers cannot get together and cut production, and the farm bill gives them a method of bringing their production down to a reasonable level and of obtaining reasonable prices for their crops." Roosevelt went on to say that if the United States could put farmers on the road to recovery, other sectors of the economy would soon follow. "It is obvious that if we can greatly increase the purchasing power of the tens of millions of our people who make a living from farming and the distribution of farm crops, we shall greatly increase the consumption of those goods which are turned out by industry."[9]

Over the next two years, the AAA had a mixed record of success. Many farmers benefited from provisions in the AAA that cut interest rates on farm mortgages. The sections of the act that sought to reduce surpluses also helped farmers who owned moderate to large amounts of acreage. The AAA has thus been credited as a key factor in the improved fortunes of the agriculture sector in the mid-1930s. By 1936, for example, commodity prices were steadily rising and many farmers had reduced their debts.

But the Act also had the unintended effect of hurting poor sharecroppers and agricultural laborers. The AAA system reduced demand for their services by reducing the total amount of land being cultivated. As a result, eviction rates of sharecroppers jumped, and competition among poor farm workers for declining work opportunities became even more desperate in many parts of the country. Finally, the idea that the government was paying farmers *not* to plant crops at a time when hunger stalked the country infuriated some Americans.

In January 1936 the controversial programs implemented through the AAA were abruptly extinguished. In the case of *United States v. Butler,* the U.S. Supreme Court ruled that the AAA was unconstitutional because it violated the rights of individual states to set their own economic rules. This decision by the conservative-dominated court outraged Roosevelt. He felt that it unfairly restricted his right, as the nation's chief executive, to regulate national commerce and agriculture. This clash was one of many that Roosevelt had with the high court during the mid-1930s.

Putting America Back to Work

The first New Deal program that explicitly addressed the nation's terrible unemployment problem was the Federal Emergency Relief Administration (FERA). This agency was created by the Federal Emergency Relief Act, which was enacted on May 22, 1933. FERA only existed until December 1935, at which point it was dissolved in favor of other unemployment and relief programs. But during its thirty months of existence, it provided jobs for an estimated 20 million Americans on public works projects across the country.

FERA was similar in many ways to New York's Temporary Emergency Relief Agency (TERA), the state relief program that Roosevelt had initiated as governor in the opening months of the Depression. Under FERA terms, states that invested in employment and welfare programs for their residents received federal matching funds that could be added to the state programs.

The agency was headed by Harry L. Hopkins, one of the most important officials of the entire New Deal (see Hopkins biography, p. 125). A skilled administrator, Hopkins recognized that if relief efforts were going to receive wide public acceptance, they had to include measures to make sure that undeserving people did not take advantage of the program. Hopkins thus made sure that all unemployment claims and requests for financial assistance were investigated. But he was also sensitive to the feelings of humiliation that many proud Americans felt about having to rely on government assistance, and he sternly punished states which he felt were not using the program's full potential.

Hopkins was deeply dedicated to the principles behind FERA in particular and the New Deal in general. "The unemployed themselves want work," he stated in late 1934. "We do not have to tell them that not having a job spoils a man for work. They go soft, they lose skill, they lose work habits. But they know it before you and I know it and it is their lives that are being wrecked, not ours.... Work for the unemployed is something we have fought for since the beginning of the administration and we shall continue to insist upon it. It preserves a man's morale. It saves his skill. It gives him a chance to do something socially useful."[10]

As the New Deal progressed, FERA paled in its influence when compared to some larger programs that followed, such as the Works Progress Administration (WPA). But despite funding limitations and its relatively short life span, the Federal Emergency Relief Administration was an important early effort of the Roosevelt White House to get victims of the Depression working again.

The National Industrial Recovery Act (NIRA)

Yet another major legislative act passed during Roosevelt's First Hundred Days was the National Industrial Recovery Act (NIRA). Enacted on June 16, 1933, this act launched two of the best-known programs of the New Deal era—the Public Works Administration (PWA) and the National Recovery Administration (NRA). NIRA also put in place new taxes on capital stocks and excess profits to pay for these ambitious programs.

Roosevelt placed the Public Works Administration under the energetic supervision of Harold L. Ickes, his Secretary of the Interior. During the next six years the PWA financed and carried out construction projects in all but

Construction workers under the direction of the Works Progress Administration work with pneumatic hammers during construction of the Grand Coulee Dam on the Columbia River.

three of the nation's 3,073 counties. These projects included seawalls, harbors, waste treatment plants and sewage systems, courthouses, housing projects, street and highway projects, hospitals, and schools. In fact, the PWA accounted for 35 percent of all new hospital and health facility construction from 1933 to 1939, and a whopping 70 percent of all new construction of education-related buildings. All told, the PWA invested more than $6 billion in projects around the country during its existence.

Ickes was a passionate champion of the PWA mission, which was to provide work opportunities for the unemployed while also tackling the nation's infrastructure needs. "Many billions of dollars could properly be spent in the United States on permanent improvements," he insisted in 1935 in *Back to Work: The Story of PWA*. "Such spending would not only help us out of the depression, it would do much for the health, well-being and prosperity of the people. I refuse to believe that providing an adequate water supply for a municipality or putting in a sewage system is a wasteful expenditure of money. Any money spent in such fashion as to make our people healthier and happier human beings is not only a good social investment, it is sound from a strictly financial point of view. I can think of no better investment, for instance, than money paid out to provide education and to safeguard the health of the people."[11]

The Blue Eagle of the NRA

The other major agency created by the National Industrial Recovery Act was the National Recovery Administration (NRA). This agency proved to be one of the most controversial—and ultimately ineffective—of Roosevelt's New Deal creations. The NRA had two goals: to improve wages and workplace conditions for workers, and to clean up some of the underhanded business practices that were hurting the economy, such as selling products at below-cost prices in order to drive smaller competitors out of business.

The NRA was placed under the direction of Hugh S. Johnson, a talented but abrasive and hard-drinking New Dealer (see Johnson biography, p. 129). Johnson and the NRA then set about enlisting the support of American business. The NRA gave industries the authority to draft their own codes of fair competition and ethics, and to set reasonable goals of profitability and levels of wage compensation. In return, participating corporations would be exempt from various federal antitrust laws limiting the power of individual companies in various industries. In addition, they would be able to display a Blue Eagle symbol on storefronts and products, which would show American consumers that the companies were patriotic participants in the NRA program.

In its early months, the NRA was embraced by Americans who were eager for deliverance from the crushing Depression. People turned out by the thousands for rallies designed to show support for the NRA, and posters of the Blue Eagle sprouted everywhere. The famous progressive newspaper editor William Allen White spoke for many leading opinion-makers when he urged his readers to cheer and support the agency. "She is no beauty," he admitted, "but, gentlemen, she has a heart of gold and good intentions, which should count for something in this wicked world."[12]

But big business used the NRA to promote its own interests rather than the economic welfare of the country as a whole. As the months passed, the NRA became the target of critics from all sides of the political spectrum. Labor unions had accepted the NRA because they had been assured that the Blue Eagle would defend labor's right to organize and negotiate with management. But the legislation that created the NRA did not provide for very severe penalties for companies that failed to bargain in good faith with unions. As corporations flouted the spirit of the agreement, labor leaders expressed rising frustration. Small businesses, meanwhile, were badly hurt in some cases by the NRA. They complained that bigger competitors used their domination of the code-drafting process to institute rules that made it more difficult for small companies to compete.

By early 1935, some critics were claiming that the initials NRA stood for "No Recovery Allowed." Johnson's fiery leadership style also came under assault from both supporters and opponents of Roosevelt's New Deal programs. It was in some ways a relief, then, when the U.S. Supreme Court declared that the National Industrial Recovery Act—which had created the NRA—was an unconstitutional violation of the Commerce Clause. This unanimous decision in *A.L.A. Schechter Poultry Corp. v. United States* was issued in May 1935. It dissolved the NRA less than two years after it had been launched with such fanfare. Roosevelt denounced the ruling because he thought that it signaled that the Court might also attack some of his other reform proposals. Many other Americans, though—including some of the New Deal's leading administrators and advocates—were not sorry to see the Blue Eagle go away.

Hugh S. Johnson (center) led the National Recovery Administration (NRA), one of the most important of Roosevelt's early New Deal agencies.

The Civilian Conservation Corps

Another federal program that appeared at about the same time as the National Recovery Administration enjoyed a much more popular run. In fact, the Civilian Conservation Corps (CCC) was the single most successful public works employment program of the entire New Deal era (see "Praise for the Civilian Conservation Corps," p. 167). Created by an executive order signed by Roosevelt on April 5, 1933, the CCC enjoyed a nine-year life. During that time, it directed the energies of more than three million young men on a tremendous array of conservation and land development projects from Florida to California. By the end of 1935 there were CCC camps in every state in the union, as well as in the Virgin Islands, Puerto Rico, and the then-territories of Alaska and Hawaii.

The CCC program took young men between 16 and 24 years old, housed them in tents and barracks, paid them $30 a month, and turned them loose on the forests, rivers, lakes, and fields of America. CCC workers planted 200 million trees, restored degraded grazing lands, built up more than 3,000 beaches, planted millions of hatchery fish in rivers and lakes, created thousands of miles of hiking trails, built hundreds of campgrounds, and fought forest fires from the northern Rockies to the Appalachians. National and state forests, federal wildlife refuges, state wildlife sanctuaries, public rangelands, historical battlefields, and parks of all shapes and sizes benefited enormously from the sweat and muscle supplied by CCC enrollees. "The billions of trees planted or protected, the millions of acres saved from the ravages of soil erosion or the depredations of flooded rivers, the hundreds of parks and recreation areas which were developed, are a permanent testimony to the success of Corps work," wrote a CCC historian. "They constitute a legitimate contribution to the heritage of every American."[13]

The CCC was headed first by Robert Fechner and then by James McEntee. They coordinated the activities of the CCC with representatives from the administration's Interior, Labor, Agriculture, and War departments. These CCC administrators benefited enormously from Roosevelt's personal enthusiasm for the program. Environmental stewardship and conservation was a high priority for Roosevelt, and he loved the idea of a program that took unemployed young men off the streets and put them hard at work in the forests and mountains. This enthusiasm made it easier

Civilian Conservation Corps workers cut wood at a CCC camp in California in 1933.

for CCC officials to obtain needed resources than administrators from other New Deal programs, who often found themselves scrambling for funding and attention.

By 1935 the CCC program was even getting kind words from people who hated other New Deal programs. Conservative Republicans who viewed other relief programs as financially irresponsible "hand outs" praised the camps for developing strong work habits and improving the nation's public resources. Local business owners close to the camps claimed that the patronage of CCC enrollees enabled them to stave off bankruptcy. And since most of the money that CCC volunteers received went to families back home, the

Ordinary Americans showed such great faith in Roosevelt, seen here with his son James, that he was able to shrug off criticism from all sides.

program provided much-needed financial assistance to millions of struggling families. By the late 1930s, politicians and community leaders were actively campaigning to host new CCC camps and projects.

In addition to all of its environmental and economic benefits, the CCC also had a major emotional impact on many of the young men who went through the program. "The CCC gave to its enrollees both a new understanding of their country and a faith in its future," explained historian John Salmond. "Youths from the teeming cities learned something of rural America, boys from farms and country hamlets became acquainted with the complexities and ethnic variation of their land and its people. Both emerged from the camp experience with a greater understanding of America, and of Americans."[14]

Renewed Hope for the Future

By the spring of 1935, many Americans felt that the New Deal policies and programs championed by Roosevelt were finally beginning to break down the economic paralysis that had gripped the country for so long. Unemployment had gradually declined to about 20 percent—still much too high, but far better than it had been when Roosevelt took office two years earlier. Some manufacturing industries were showing signs of revival as well. From 1932 to 1935, for example, sales of automobiles in the United States jumped from 1.1 million to 3.8 million. Finally, New Deal relief programs had begun making progress in reducing hunger and homelessness.

Importantly, Roosevelt had convinced most Americans to take his side in the feverish debate over the "American-ness" of his New Deal policies. Some conservative critics charged that his relief programs—and even his work programs, in which people were paid to work on public projects—threatened to create a generation of lazy and unmotivated wards of the state. But most Americans rejected this argument.

Ironically, during this same period some liberal critics condemned Roosevelt and his New Dealers for not going *far enough* in their relief efforts. They charged that despite all of Roosevelt's rhetoric, his highest priority was really to preserve the privileged lives of affluent Americans who had escaped the worst effects of the Depression. In 1934, for example, a delegation of unemployed workers marched into the offices of FERA Director Harry L. Hopkins and proclaimed that "we want you to know that we have no faith in you. We are well aware that your policy is not to relieve the unemployed, but to stretch out relief thinly enough to save the incomes of the rich, at the same time that you give enough to prevent an uprising of the workers."[15] But most Americans rejected this characterization of the Roosevelt administration as well.

Finally, Roosevelt persuaded the great majority of Americans that the expanded presence of the federal government in their daily lives did not pose a threat to their personal freedom, as conservative critics charged. Instead, they accepted Roosevelt's explanation that increased federal involvement in economic matters was a matter of necessity, and that it was being done to restore happiness and prosperity to beleaguered Americans. "Answer this question out of the facts of your own life," he asked a nationwide audience during a June 1934 fireside chat. "Have you lost any of your rights or liberty or constitutional freedom of action and choice?" Roosevelt then urged his listeners to read the Bill of Rights "and ask yourself whether you personally have suffered the impairment of a single jot of these great assurances. I have no question in my mind as to what your answer will be. The record is written in the experiences of your own personal lives."[16]

Notes:

[1] Smiley, Gene. *Rethinking the Great Depression.* Chicago: Ivan R. Dee, 2002, pp. 28-9.

[2] Roosevelt, Franklin D., Inaugural Address, March 4, 1933, from The American Presidency Project, http://www.presidency.ucsb.edu.

[3] Quoted in Turkel, Studs. *Hard Times: An Oral History of the Great Depression,* New York: Pantheon, 1971.

[4] Quoted in Dallek, Robert. *Franklin D. Roosevelt and American Foreign Policy, 1932-1945.* New York: Oxford University Press, 1979, p. 35.

[5] McCormick Anne O'Hare. *The World at Home: Selections from the Writings of Anne O'Hare McCormick.* Edited by Marion Turner Sheehan. 1956. New York: Books for Libraries, 1970, p. 176.

[6] Watkins, T.H. *The Hungry Years: A Narrative History of the Great Depression in America.* New York: Owl Books, 2000, p. 152.

[7] Parrish, Michael. *Anxious Decades: America in Prosperity and Depression.* New York: Norton, 1992, p. 299.

8 Egan, Timothy. *The Worst Hard Time.* Boston: Houghton Mifflin, 2006, p. 133.

9 Roosevelt, Franklin D., Fireside Chat, July 24, 1933, from *The American Presidency Project,* http: //www.presidency.ucsb.edu.

10 Hopkins, Harry L. Radio address, Dec. 31, 1934. Reprinted in *Vital Speeches of the Day.* New York, 1934, pp. 210-12.

11 Ickes, Harold. *Back to Work: The Story of PWA.* New York: Macmillan, 1935.

12 Quoted in Watkins, p. 198.

13 Salmond, John A. Chapter 13 of *The Civilian Conservation Corps, 1933-1942: A New Deal Case Study.* Durham, NC: Duke University Press, 1967. Available online at www.nps.gov/history/history /online_books/ccc/salmond/chap13.htm

14 Salmond, ch. 13.

15 Gambs, John S., "United We Eat," *Survey Graphic,* August 1934, p. 357.

16 Roosevelt, Franklin D. Fireside chat, June 28, 1934, from The American Presidency Project, http: //www.presidency.ucsb.edu.

Chapter Four

THE DUST BOWL

<hr/>

The land just blew away. We had to go somewhere.
—Kansas minister on the road to California, June 1936

When the Roosevelt administration unleashed its initial flurry of New Deal programs in 1933 and 1934, it knew that it faced an enormous challenge. It had to simultaneously save victims of the Great Depression from hunger, poverty, and hopelessness; help unemployed Americans return to work; aid cash-starved businesses in their quest to regain profitability; and restore shaken public faith in American-style capitalism. But even as Roosevelt was setting his New Deal in motion, yet another threat to the nation emerged on the Great Plains. This threat—popularly known as the Dust Bowl—had the potential to turn much of the country's agricultural heartland into a bleak desert. It also complicated Roosevelt's entire strategy for battling the Great Depression.

The Farming Boom

During the first quarter of the twentieth century, American farmers on the Great Plains—a broad cross-section of the central United States that includes parts of Colorado, Kansas, Montana, Nebraska, New Mexico, Oklahoma, North Dakota, South Dakota, Texas, and Wyoming—had enjoyed steadily rising levels of prosperity. They had endured occasional years of poor production or sagging prices, but most of the years had been good ones. Conditions in the post-World War I era, in particular, lifted many farmers to new heights of success. There were two main reasons for this growth. First, by the time the war concluded in 1918, European agriculture was in ruins. This forced European nations to look overseas for their food. Second, U.S. consumers dramatically increased their consumption of wheat, corn, meat, and other agricultural products during the economic expansion of the 1920s.

American farmers and ranchers expanded their operations and production to meet the soaring demand. The Great Plains even received an infusion of new farmers eager to take advantage of the high prices for various commodities. Wheat was the single most important economic crop during this time, but other commodities surged in commercial value as well.

During the late 1920s, though, the picture changed. Heartland producers of wheat, cotton, corn, and pigs found themselves in deepening financial straits. They watched helplessly as prices for farm commodities steadily fell in response to the recovery of European farming. This recovery, combined with the record output of American growers, created a glut of wheat and other crops on the world market. Prices continued to fall, and many farmers who had taken out big loans to buy new machinery or land during the early 1920s fell deeper and deeper into debt. Commodity prices further plummeted after the Stock Market Crash of 1929, which ushered in the Great Depression.

The position of farmers and ranchers of the Great Plains further eroded in the early 1930s, when the weather turned against them. In 1933 and 1934, many parts of the Great Plains received record-low levels of rainfall. Drought conditions became so bad that some reservoirs, creeks, and ponds disappeared entirely, while lakes, marshes, and rivers shriveled to a fraction of their former sizes. The drought decimated regional populations of fish, amphibian, and bird species—but created ideal conditions for grasshoppers, which hatched in plague-like numbers and devoured the meager crops that farmers could coax from the ground.

The impact of the drought years was made worse by the fact that day after day, the sun was blazing down on fields and rangelands that had been treated very poorly for decades. By 1930, overgrazing by cattle and sheep had transformed many rangelands into fields of stubbled dirt. Land cultivated for crop production was in even worse condition. Millions of acres of Great Plains grasslands had been repeatedly plowed up to plant wheat and other crops. Ignoring farming principles that would have allowed these soils to recover, farmers instead used the fields so intensively that soil nutrients were exhausted and topsoil became intensely vulnerable to erosion. "At the end of

1931, the Agriculture College of Oklahoma did a survey of all the land that had been torn up in their state during the wheat bonanza," said one historian. "They were astonished by what they found: of sixteen million acres in cultivation in the state, thirteen million were seriously eroded. And this was before the drought had calcified most of the ground."[1]

Era of the Dusters

The stage was thus set for the greatest natural disaster in the history of the United States. In the early 1930s the steady winds that were a regular feature of life on the Great Plains began picking up the shattered, sun-baked topsoil and carrying it miles away. Huge dust storms rolled across parts of Kansas, Nebraska, Colorado, New Mexico, Texas, and the Oklahoma panhandle. These "dusters" blotted out the mid-day sun and heaved massive dunes of dirt against the sides of homes, barns, and silos. "It seemed on many days as if a curtain was being drawn across a vast stage at world's end," wrote one historian:

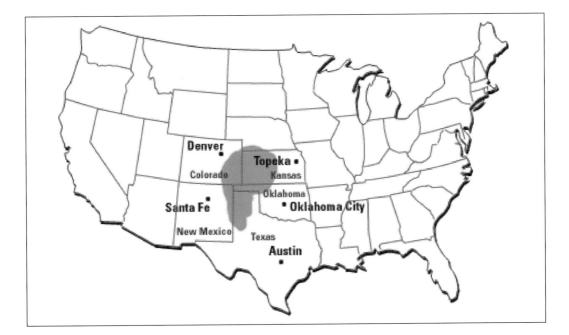

The Dust Bowl spread across portions of five states, and was felt to a lesser degree in several other states across the Great Plains.

> The land convulsed in a way that had never been seen before, and it did so at a time when one out of every four adults was out of work.... Cattle went blind and suffocated. When farmers cut them open, they found stomachs stuffed with fine sand. Horses ran madly against the storms. Children coughed and gagged, dying of something the doctors called "dust pneumonia." In desperation, some families gave away their children. The instinctive act of hugging a loved one or shaking someone's hand could knock two people down, for the static electricity from the dusters was so strong.[2]

People who lived through the Dust Bowl recalled that farming families were completely at the mercy of the dust and wind. "The fields were just blowing away," recalled one Kansan. "I know my dad used a harrow, just to turn the ground over so it wouldn't blow so hard. And, he didn't always shave everyday and he'd come in with that dust just hanging on those short whiskers, his face was just covered in dirt.... A few years later, a lot of farmers died with emphysema and there was just plain dust in their lungs."[3]

Farmhouses and schools did not provide any refuge from the maddening dust, either. People caked their nostrils with Vaseline to catch the dust as they inhaled, and many elementary schools received boxes of respiratory masks from the Red Cross. Families draped damp bed sheets across closed windows overnight, only to awake in the morning to find them caked in a brown paste.

Even the simple act of eating turned into a test of resolve and ingenuity during the Dust Bowl years. "Women learned to put up water and milk in tightly sealed Mason jars at the first sign of a storm so that the liquids would not become an undrinkable sludge," reported one historian. "When the time came to use the jars, holes were punched in the tops and the drinks were sucked up through straws.... Everything was eaten the instant it left the stove in the few precious moments before grime covered it. Even so, dust was ingested like a condiment with every meal."[4]

As drought conditions persisted, crops withered, and the dusters rolled on, many of the people trapped in the Dust Bowl became demoralized. "The area seems doomed to become in dreary reality the Great American Desert shown on early maps," wrote one desperate Kansas wheat farmer. "This was something new and different from anything I had ever experienced before—a

Dusters turned many American farms into desert landscapes in the space of a few short years.

destroying force beyond my wildest imagination." And over time, the conditions took a physical as well as psychological toll. "The dust I … labored in all day began to show its effects on my system," he continued. "My head ached, my stomach was upset, and my lungs were oppressed and felt as if they must contain a ton of fine dirt."[5]

Black Sunday

On a number of occasions from 1933 through 1936, the daily gusts of wind-blown dust built up into full-fledged dust storms that blackened the

63

The worst of the dust storms that smothered America's Great Plains during the Depression was the Black Sunday storm of April 14, 1935.

skies over the Great Plains. A few of these storms were so gigantic that they deposited dirt from the Dakotas and Kansas and Oklahoma on windshields in New York City. Even ships hundreds of miles out in the Atlantic Ocean were coated with dust from the Great Plains.

But one of these storms was more fearsome than all the rest. This storm took place on April 14, 1935, and terrorized residents of five states—Nebraska, Colorado, Kansas, Texas, and Oklahoma—before blowing out into the Gulf of Mexico. The storm was so spectacular in its fury that the day in which it hit became forever known as "Black Sunday" in the folklore of the Great Plains (see "Remembering 'Black Sunday,'" p. 179).

The Black Sunday dust storm began in the drought-stricken Dakotas in the early morning hours and gathered strength with each passing mile. In county after county, a great wall of black blotted out the northern horizon, carrying tens of thousands of tons of topsoil lifted from the pulverized farmlands over which it passed. By the time the storm reached the northern borders of Colorado and Kansas, it was a vast and roiling black curtain that measured hundreds of miles across.

As the duster enveloped each town and farmhouse in its path, sunlight was extinguished so totally that people caught in the storm could not even see their hands. Radios and car ignitions shorted out in the static-charged storm, and roads vanished under waves of sand and dirt. Livestock caught out in the open choked to death on the flying dust, and barbed wire fences glowed with electricity. Frightened people gathered together in darkened churches and living rooms and openly debated whether the end of the world was at hand. And in a small town in Texas, a young folk singer named Woody Guthrie composed the opening lines of one of his most famous songs—"So Long, It's Been Good to Know Yuh"—as the Black Sunday storm roared over his head.[6] (See "Woody Guthrie Describes the Dust Bowl," p. 176).

To Stay or Go

For some residents of the Great Plains, the nightmarish events of Black Sunday convinced them to follow neighbors that had already fled the region. For these unfortunate souls, the poverty and hopelessness simply became too much for them to bear. Visitors to the Dust Bowl did not blame them for leaving. One observer passing through Kansas expressed shock that "in America it should take just one generation to reduce its prolific nature to a condition like the Gobi Desert, which was a million years in the making."[7] The famous journalist Ernie Pyle offered a similar assessment of conditions when he toured the Dust Bowl in 1935. He reported that in many parts of the countryside he "saw not a solitary thing but bare earth and a few lonely, empty farmhouses… There was not a tree or a blade of grass, or a dog or a cow or a human being—nothing whatsoever, nothing at all but gray raw earth and a few farmhouses and barns, sticking up from the dark gray sea like white cattle skeletons on the desert.… [It was] the saddest land I have ever seen."[8]

"This was something new and different from anything I had ever experienced before—a destroying force beyond my wildest imagination," recalled one farmer. "My head ached, my stomach was upset, and my lungs were oppressed and felt as if they must contain a ton of fine dirt."

Yet the majority of people who lived in the Dust Bowl never left. Instead, they endured with the help of friends and family—and by nurturing their flickering confidence that the rain would someday return. Many of them also stayed because they knew that the people who lived in the big cities had their own problems. "They saw the newsreels in the Mission Theater in Dalhart [Texas] and the Palace in Boise City [Idaho], showing those breadlines in the big cities, the apple vendors on every street corner, the millions crying for relief," explained historian Timothy Egan. "At least here, in a cashless economy, people could squeeze a dozen eggs every day from a house of hens, or get a pail of milk from an old cow, or spread waters from the windmill onto the ground to grow vegetables, or fatten up a pig, then smoke a winter's supply of bacon."[9]

California-Bound

The people who did decide to leave the Dust Bowl set their sights on many different parts of the country. Some drifted to the homes of family members back east or in the Deep South. Most African-American refugees from the Dust Bowl set their sights on Chicago, Detroit, Boston, New York, and other northern cities, where discrimination and anti-black violence was not as pervasive as it was in the Jim Crow South. For the majority of people who left the Dust Bowl, though, the destination was California.

As many as 400,000 Oklahomans, Texans, Arkansans, and Missourians moved to California during the 1930s.[10] Some of them made a fairly painless transition to life in California. People who had previously lived in towns or small cities and supported themselves through factory work or white-collar occupations were better equipped financially to make the move, and they also had skills that were in greater demand. But relocating farm families faced a much different set of circumstances. Their stories, documented in the photographs of Dorothea Lange and dramatized in the John Steinbeck novel *The Grapes of Wrath,* are the ones that became most closely associated with the Dust Bowl exodus. In fact, the refugees' desperate flight to California came to symbolize the entire Great Depression era in the minds of future generations of Americans (see "An Excerpt from John Steinbeck's *The Grapes of Wrath*," p. 170).

The attraction of California to these refugees was clear. For one thing, California had a unique reputation among most Americans as a virtual Eden—blessed with a pleasing climate, beautiful country, and a wealth of nat-

This 1936 Dorothea Lange photograph of a Dust Bowl victim with three small children became one of the most famous images of the entire Great Depression era.

ural riches. "Born amidst the frenzy of the [1849] Gold Rush, the state had ever since sustained a reputation as a place where fortunes were made, where opportunities abounded," wrote one Dust Bowl historian. "Come to California to find the 'good life,' Americans were told. And come they did."[11]

The other aspect of California that drew refugees from the farms of Oklahoma and other Dust Bowl states was its ranking as the nation's leading producer of agricultural products. In the 1930s California contained more than 40 percent of the nation's large-scale dairy farms and more than half of its large poultry farms. In addition, the state's San Joaquin, San Bernardino, and Sacramento valleys raised huge volumes of cotton, oranges, grapes, and other crops. The existence of these massive farms was tremendously reassuring to migrant families who were unfamiliar with any other kind of life but one that was based on agriculture.

The journey to the promised land of California, though, was a brutal one for many. Thousands of individuals and families were completely impoverished by the time they departed the Dust Bowl. They piled all of their worldly belongings into old automobiles and trucks that labored mightily as they crawled westward. At night they huddled off Route 66 and other highways in makeshift camps, where they sometimes combined their meager meals with those of other refugee families. The loneliness and uncertainty that accompanied these journeys was heightened by the hostile reception that the refugees sometimes received at towns and homesteads along the way. Many Americans were anxious about keeping their jobs and about conserving their own limited resources, and they saw the Dust Bowl refugees as potential threats to both of those things.

Still, the refugees pressed onward to California with grit and determination—and the occasional helpful hand from strangers. Flossie Haggard, mother of country music singer Merle Haggard, was one of many who left the Dust Bowl for California. Years later, she recalled the desperation she felt when her family's old car broke down in the desert. "We were out of water, and just when I thought we weren't going to make it, I saw this boy coming down the highway on a bicycle. He was going all the way from Kentucky to Fresno. He shared a quart of water with us and helped us fix the car. Everybody's been treating us like trash, and I told this boy, 'I'm glad to see there's still some decent folks left in this world.'"[12] Other travelers survived by clinging to a stubborn optimism about the future that awaited them. "To most of the refugees hope is greater than obstacles," wrote a journalist in a 1935 issue of *Survey Graphic*. "With

Miserable tent shelters such as this one often provided the only protection from the elements for migrant agricultural workers and their families.

bedding drenched by rain while he slept in the open, with topless car and a tire gone flat, an Oklahoman with the usual numerous dependents could say, 'Pretty hard on us now. Sun'll come out pretty soon and we'll be all right.'"[13]

A Cold Reception

The Dust Bowl refugees who straggled into California came to be collectively known as "Okies"—an abbreviation for the word Oklahomans. It did not take long for the term to take on an insulting meaning among Californians. They resented the intrusion of these poor white migrants into their state, which was already struggling with the economic tumult of the Depression. One columnist in the *Los Angeles Times* was so upset about the influx of Okies that he expressed bitterness about the high quality of southern California's highways: "The Chinese, wiser than we, have delayed building a great system of highways for that very reason—to head off these dangerous migrations—indigent people stampeding from the farms into cities to live on charity."[14]

The arrival of the refugees was greeted with particular hostility by the agricultural laborers already working in the state. They knew that the migrants from the Great Plains would make it harder for them to find jobs—and easier for the big farms to cut wages for field work. In addition, Mexican Americans and other minorities within the agricultural labor force feared that the increased competition for jobs would set off new waves of racist violence against them. This fear proved well-founded. As the Depression dragged on, whites in several California communities attacked minority workers with guns, clubs, and dynamite to keep them away from even poor-paying jobs.

The Okies also received the cold shoulder from members of California's middle class and upper class. City leaders feared that if migrant laborers stayed too long, their communities would be forced to add them to their already overtaxed relief programs. This concern led some towns and cities to mount organized campaigns against the "intruders." In 1936, for example, the Los Angeles police department established a border patrol that came to be known as the "bum blockade." These officers set up checkpoints at major road and rail crossings and refused to let people into the city if they could not show evidence that they had money or a job.

California legislators also passed the 1933 Indigent Act, which made it a crime to bring needy and jobless people into the state (other states passed similar laws during the Depression in an effort to keep the poor and homeless from crossing their borders). In the late 1930s this law was used to prosecute several Californians who helped Dust Bowl relatives move into the state. It remained on the books until 1941, when the U.S. Supreme Court ruled in *Edwards v. California* that states had no right to restrict interstate migration by poor people or any other Americans.

Despite all these hurdles, however, most Dust Bowl refugees eventually managed to carve out lives for themselves in the unfamiliar valleys and towns of California. Working in orchards, canneries, factories, offices, and cotton fields, they gradually managed to get back on their economic feet. Federal relief programs helped individuals and families as well. Their fortunes further improved in the early 1940s, when American involvement in World War II triggered economic growth throughout the country. This economic expansion enabled many migrants from the Great Plains to obtain better-paying jobs in a wide assortment of industries.

Restoring a Broken Land

Back on the Great Plains, meanwhile, the federal government launched a frantic campaign to restore the shattered region. One of the weapons the Roosevelt administration used was the Taylor Grazing Act of 1934, which placed new restrictions on grazing on some public lands in the West. One year later, Roosevelt created the Resettlement Administration, which provided loans and other assistance to Great Plains farming families that wanted to relocate. He also signed an executive order granting the federal government powers to buy western land back from homesteaders.

The leading force in the effort to save the Great Plains, though, was the Soil Conservation Service. This was an agency within the Department of Agriculture that was created in 1935 by Congressional passage of the Soil Conservation Act. The Soil Conservation Service was led by Hugh Hammond Bennett, a scientist with the Department of Agriculture. Bennett had issued strong warnings about the farming practices used on the Great Plains as far back as the 1920s. In 1928, for example, Bennett and W.R. Chapline co-authored a study called *Soil Erosion: A National Menace*. In this report, Bennett bluntly predicted that "an era of land wreckage destined to weigh heavily upon the welfare of the next generation is at hand."[15]

Bennett benefited greatly from the support of Secretary of Agriculture Henry Wallace, who also believed that Americans had become wasteful, irresponsible users of farmland and other natural resources (see Wallace biography, p. 148). Wallace, for example, reassigned more than 500 units of the Civilian Conservation Corps (CCC) to Bennett's agency to serve as foot soldiers in the battle to restore the vitality of the Great Plains.

When Bennett took command of the Soil Conservation Service in 1935, he funneled most of the agency's resources into two areas. The first was to restore sections of ruined land by planting natural grasses, establishing "greenbelts" of new trees to break up the momentum of Plains winds, and acquiring farmlands that would be left alone so they could replenish themselves. Bennett was greatly aided in these efforts by CCC volunteers. The second area of focus was to educate farmers about sustainable agriculture practices and organize them into cooperative "conservation districts." More than

John Steinbeck and *The Grapes of Wrath*

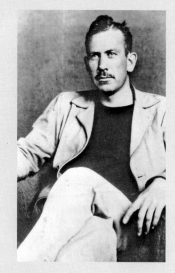

John Ernst Steinbeck was born in Salinas, California, on February 27, 1902. The son of a county administrator and a school teacher, Steinbeck spent much of his childhood and teen years reading literature and working on area ranches. He attended college at Stanford University, but left in the mid-1920s without a degree in order to pursue a writing career in New York City. He returned to California a few years later and lived there for most of the rest of his life.

Steinbeck published a number of novels in the late 1920s and early 1930s, but *Tortilla Flat* (1935) and *Of Mice and Men* (1936) were the first to attract significant critical acclaim. In 1936 Steinbeck's attention was drawn to the struggles of Dust Bowl refugees who were pouring into California at that time. After penning several newspaper articles on their plight, Steinbeck

2,000 of these districts were eventually established encompassing more than 200 million acres. District members implemented new, more environmentally sustainable methods of plowing, planting, and irrigating. Bennett also convinced members of these districts to stop looking at the regions they worked as checkerboards of adjoining lands with no relationship to one another. Bennett's crusade received an additional boost with the 1936 creation of the Agricultural Conservation Program (ACP). This program paid farmers to replace seven soil-depleting crops, including corn, cotton, and wheat, with soil-conserving grasses and cover crops.

All of these strategies had the ultimate goal of convincing farmers of the wisdom of managing their lands together as a single large ecological unit. "Ours was a new type of program in which success depended on making use of all available and effective measures of control, singly or in combination, as needed in order to establish durable conservation on all the land," Bennett

decided to devote an entire novel to their struggles. *The Grapes of Wrath* was published three years later, and it was an immediate sensation with readers from coast to coast.

The Grapes of Wrath tells the story of Tom Joad and his family. As the novel progresses, the Joads lose their Oklahoma farm in the Dust Bowl, fight to reach California, and then confront numerous hardships in their newly adopted homeland. Steinbeck's novel was immediately hailed as a masterpiece of American literature, and it has shaped perceptions of the entire Depression era for multiple generations of readers. In 1940 director John Ford released a film version of the Steinbeck novel. This movie, also called *The Grapes of Wrath,* starred Henry Fonda as Tom Joad and was a huge critical and popular success.

After *The Grapes of Wrath*, Steinbeck published several other popular, highly-praised literary works, including *The Pearl* (1947) and *East of Eden* (1952). During World War II Steinbeck served as a war correspondent for the *New York Herald Tribune.*

He received the Nobel Prize for Literature in 1962. He died six years later in New York City, on December 20, 1968.

later wrote. "I consider the soil conservation districts movement one of the most important developments in the whole history of agriculture."[16]

Historians agree that the programs implemented by the Soil Conservation Service in the 1930s played a hugely important role in the gradual recovery of large tracts of Great Plains farmland. Another big factor was a return to more normal rainfall levels in the late 1930s. In addition, farmers became less vulnerable to drought as advances in scientific knowledge and new well-drilling technology gave them increased access to vast underground aquifers.

Still, some scholars believe that Great Plains farmers and government agencies never fully embraced the land conservation ideals for which Bennett and Wallace fought. Historians point out that although the Roosevelt administration originally intended to take 75 million acres of Great Plains farmland out of production, only 11 million acres were ever purchased. And although some of this acreage was eventually designated as National Grasslands and allowed to revert to a wild state, other parts of the former Dust Bowl remained intensely vulnerable to exploitative, destructive farming practices in post-World War II America.

Notes:

[1] Egan, Timothy. *The Worst Hard Time.* Boston: Houghton Mifflin, 2006, p. 111.

[2] Egan, pp. 2, 5.

[3] Crum, Lola Adams, Interview with Brandon Case, June 23, 1998. *Ford County Dust Bowl Oral History Project,* Ford County Historical Society, Dodge City, KS, http://skyways.lib.ks.us/orgs/fordco/dustbowl.

[4] Watkins, T.H. *The Hungry Years: A Narrative History of the Great Depression in America.* New York: Owl Books, 2000, p. 428.

[5] Svobida, Lawrence. *Farming the Dust Bowl: A First-Hand Account from Kansas.* Reprint. Originally published as *An Empire of Dust,* 1940. Lawrence: University Press of Kansas, 1986, pp. 59, 195.

[6] Egan, pp. 220-21.

[7] Quoted in Lowitt, Richard. *The New Deal and the West.* Bloomington, IN: Indiana University Press, 1984, p. 35.

[8] Quoted in Egan, p. 256.

[9] Egan, p. 111.

[10] Gregory, James N. "The Dust Bowl Migration: Poverty Stories, Race Stories." In *American Exodus: The Dust Bowl Migration and Okie Culture in California,* [companion website], available online at http://faculty.washington.edu/gregoryj/exodus/.

[11] Quoted in Gregory, James, *American Exodus: The Dust Bowl Migration and Okie Culture in California.* New York: Oxford University Press, 1989, pp. 7, 8.

[12] Quoted in Gregory, *American Exodus,* p. 34.

[13] Taylor, Paul, "Again the Covered Wagon," *Survey Graphic,* July 1935, p. 348.

[14] Taylor, p. 348.

[15] Bennett, Hugh Hammond, and W.R. Chapline. *Soil Erosion: A National Menace.* U.S. Department of Agriculture Circular No. 33. Washington, DC: U.S. Government Printing Office, 1928, p. 22.

[16] Bennett, Hugh Hammond. *The Hugh Bennett Lectures.* Raleigh, NC: The Agricultural Foundation, North Carolina State College, June 1959, pp. 25, 28.

Chapter Five

THE SECOND NEW DEAL

Governments can err—Presidents do make mistakes.... [But] better the occasional faults of a government that lives in a spirit of charity than the consistent omissions of a government frozen in the ice of its own indifference.

—President Franklin D. Roosevelt, 1936

At the same time that President Roosevelt and his fellow New Dealers were battling the horrors of the Dust Bowl, they were also preparing a host of new social and economic programs to combat other aspects of the Depression. In 1935, in fact, the Roosevelt administration launched what came to be widely known as the Second New Deal. During this time, Roosevelt signed the Social Security Act, one of the most important and far-reaching pieces of legislation in American history. He also started the Works Progress Administration (WPA), which employed millions of Americans during the Depression. Another milestone was the 1935 National Labor Relations Act, which gave labor unions important new rights. The popularity of these initiatives helped Roosevelt win re-election in 1936.

During this same period, however, Roosevelt became an extremely unpopular figure in some parts of America. Some activists, politicians, and ordinary Americans with strong liberal or socialist beliefs claimed that he was not doing enough for poor and working-class families. But the greatest hostility came from the political right. Many corporate interests and conservative Americans came to see him as an enemy of business and a threat to beloved ideals of freedom and independence. These accusations intensified in late 1937 and 1938, when the American economy—

which had seemed to be on the road to recovery—fell into another frightening downturn.

Navigating Fierce Political Storms

Two years into the Roosevelt presidency, the majority of Americans believed that the administration was making slow but steady progress in beating back the Great Depression. But the economic news remained grim in many parts of the country, and stories of heartache, anxiety, and desperation still dominated newspapers and kitchen-table conversations. "We were a close knit neighborhood and everybody tried to help their neighbor if they had problems," recalled a woman who grew up on an Idaho farm during the Depression:

> The thing that I noticed most, that I remember most, was how many people needed jobs. They call them bums that came on the railroad, and they bring what they had on their backs, and come and ask for a day's work; and if you fed them, they'd work for nothing, so you'd just feed them. You could hire all kinds of men for a dollar a day. And some of them would say, "If you keep me, I'll stay for the winter." If you just give them a bed and food. And if you had a job, and you didn't take care of it, there was a half a dozen waiting for your job. If you had a job you was mighty happy ... to keep it.[1]

During the mid-1930s, several radical voices emerged out of this atmosphere of fear and uncertainty to become powerful political forces. One was Francis Townsend, a doctor who proposed to distribute $200 monthly payments to every American over the age of 60. The "Townsend Plan," which proposed new sales taxes to raise money for these payments, was hugely popular. At its height, about two million Americans joined so-called Townsend Clubs to support the plan. Townsend's proposed sales tax, however, would not have come close to paying for the senior citizen payments. In the end, the movement collapsed under the weight of its unrealistic economic foundations.

Another radical figure was Charles Coughlin, a Catholic priest based in suburban Detroit. Coughlin's national radio broadcasts in the late 1920s and early 1930s made him a prominent national figure. When Roosevelt launched his New Deal in 1933, Coughlin voiced his support because he thought it would improve wages and conditions for working men and women. But within a year he turned against the New Deal. Convinced that Roosevelt's programs were tainted by Communist ideas, he attacked the New Deal again and again in sermons and radio speeches. Coughlin even declared that Roosevelt had built an unholy alliance with Jews, whom the fiercely anti-Semitic priest blamed for all kinds of problems in America and around the world.

The most powerful voice to emerge out of the anger and sadness of the Great Depression, though, belonged to Huey Long. The "Kingfish," as Long was known throughout his native Louisiana, rose to national prominence during the Hoover years. After winning the governorship of Louisiana in 1928 as a Democrat, Long consolidated virtually all of the state's political power in his office. He was able to get away with this because of the various reforms he passed to improve the lives of the state's many poor citizens. Long's policies were matched by his rhetoric. Time and again, he condemned corporate executives as greedy slavemasters and promised that with his leadership, every working man could be a king.

Louisiana politician Huey Long became one of the most popular—and controversial—politicians in the United States during the Depression.

In 1932 Long easily won election to the U.S. Senate, where he repeatedly called for massive redistributions of wealth in America. He warned that if his prescription for change was not heeded, the United States might slide into another civil war. This sort of talk alarmed Roosevelt, who privately described the senator from Louisiana as one of the most dangerous men in the country. It also disgusted and angered Republicans, corporate executives, and many middle-class Americans who thought that Long was just adding to the nation's social and economic turmoil.

Many poor Americans, though, were attracted to Long's message. When he formed a Share Our Wealth Society to advance his political and economic agendas in 1934, millions of people signed up. Long's Share Our Wealth movement demanded that the U.S. government take the fortunes of America's wealthiest families and distribute the money to the poor and needy. In addition, Long called for legislation that would use government programs to keep all Americans out of poverty, limit the personal fortunes that people could acquire, and fund ambitious education and public works initiatives. The Louisiana senator also talked openly about challenging Roosevelt for the Democratic presidential nomination in 1936.

In 1935 Roosevelt took steps to address the public anger that propelled the growth of the Share Our Wealth movement—and to increase government revenue for his various New Deal programs. At the beginning of the summer, he called on Congress to impose new taxes on inherited wealth, corporate profits, and high-income Americans. Targets of the new taxes immediately condemned Roosevelt's proposal as a "soak-the-rich" scheme, and opponents managed to water down the bill. Still, the 1935 Wealth Tax Act did increase taxes on the nation's wealthiest members and place new taxes on corporate profits and large inheritances.

The Wealth Tax Act was passed on August 30. Less than two weeks later, Long's colorful political career was cut short by violence. On September 8, 1935, he was shot in Louisiana by the son-in-law of one of his political foes. When the Kingfish died two days later from his wounds, the poor, rural Americans that supported him went into mourning. But many other people were secretly—or not so—secretly-relieved by his death.

The Works Progress Administration

The Wealth Tax Act was one element of what many historians describe as Roosevelt's Second New Deal, which was unfurled during the spring and summer of 1935 (see "Roosevelt Unveils the Second New Deal," p. 189). Unlike the first slate of New Deal programs, which focused more on fixing institutional problems within the American economy, this flurry of new programs and laws was designed to lift up ailing families and increase consumer spending.

One of the most important of these 1935 initiatives was Roosevelt's creation (by executive order) of the Works Progress Administration (WPA) on May 6. This new agency was similar in many ways to the Public Works Administration (PWA), the administration's two-year-old effort to put unemployed Americans back to work building schools, hospitals, airports, dams, and other public works. But unlike the PWA, which provided financing to

A trainee operates machinery at a WPA training center in Chicago.

private companies for such projects, the WPA handled all aspects of the projects from start to finish.

The WPA was headed by Harry L. Hopkins, who took the works division of the Federal Emergency Relief Administration (FERA) and reshaped it to his needs. He put together a network of local, regional, and state offices, all of which reported to Hopkins in Washington, D.C. Over the six-year life of the WPA, it put a broad cross-section of Americans to work. Engineers, welders, plumbers, construction workers, and other people in the building trades were the greatest beneficiaries. But the WPA also launched programs that helped thousands of playwrights, photographers, painters, musicians, dancers, teachers, writers, seamstresses, and academic researchers to survive the grim economic times. "My father immediately got employed in this WPA," recalled one woman who lived through the Depression. "This was a godsend. This was the greatest thing. It meant food, you know. Survival, just survival."[2]

Throughout the life of the WPA, Roosevelt, Hopkins, and many other New Dealers praised the agency—which provided jobs for more than eight million Americans—as one of the noblest successes of their Depression-fighting campaign. "Every time a man is taken from the demoralizing ranks of the jobless, every time a woman is removed from the humiliation of a breadline, and given work to do, a home somewhere becomes more secure," said WPA official Ellen Woodward. "This, in a word, is the first aim of the Works Progress Administration: To put destitute people at work at familiar tasks, that their moral fiber may not be undermined and their hopes and ambitions killed, by the forced acceptance of public charity in the form of a dole."[3]

Still, the WPA was not universally loved. Some workers expressed frustration and anger about the low wages that most WPA projects offered. The administration kept wages down, however, because they did not want labor unions to see the WPA as a threat to their membership drives. In addition, Hopkins wanted to make sure that once America's economic picture brightened, WPA workers would be motivated to move on to jobs in the private sector.

Critics also complained that WPA workers were lazy "shovel leaners" who did not take pride in their workmanship. Political opponents of the New Deal were particularly quick to level this charge. Stories of WPA workers taking afternoon naps or hour-long coffee breaks were frequently traded among Americans who disliked Roosevelt and his policies.

These claims, though, were not supported by the sheer magnitude of what the WPA accomplished. In fact, the Works Progress Administration completed a mind-boggling array of major projects during its existence. It built or renovated more than 110,000 schools, public libraries, stadiums, and auditoriums. It built 256 new airports, 880 sewage treatment plants, and 770 municipal swimming pools. The agency also constructed more than 75,000 bridges and viaducts, built or repaired 1.2 million miles of culverts, and poured concrete for 24,000 miles of sidewalks. In addition, WPA projects built or repaired an estimated 600,000 miles of highways, streets, and roads. Moreover, the WPA funded thousands of theatrical performances, concerts, circuses, documentary projects, and other efforts that greatly enriched the nation's artistic and educational life.[4]

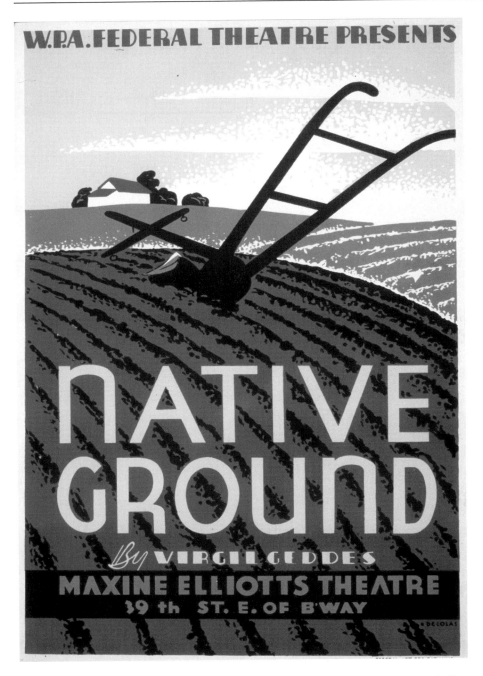

Poster for a WPA theatrical production at Maxine Elliotts Theatre in New York City.

Finally, the WPA marked an important milestone in the efforts of African Americans to claim something more than the economic crumbs left by whites. When Roosevelt signed the executive order that created the WPA in May 1935, he declared that all individuals who "qualified by training and experience to be assigned to [WPA] work projects shall not be discriminated against on any grounds whatsoever."[5] This directive was obeyed by Hopkins and other top WPA officials, who worked hard to ensure that African Americans benefited from the program. This was an enormous challenge in rural parts of the Deep South. The remote setting of these regions, where white racism remained rampant, made it difficult to enforce the anti-discrimination provisions in the WPA's charter. But African-American enrollment in the WPA was high in many Southern cities, as well as across the North and in the West. The economic lifeline that these jobs provided was not forgotten by African Americans, who became steadfast supporters of Roosevelt.

The Social Security Act

Another pillar of the Second New Deal was the Social Security Act, which Roosevelt signed into law in August 1935. Efforts to establish a national pension system for older Americans had been pursued since the early twentieth century. Until the Great Depression, these proposals had always been blocked by powerful business interests who did not want to pay higher taxes for such a program. But the Great Depression plunged so many elderly Americans into poverty that the drive for some sort of pension program took on new urgency. Advocates such as Townsend and novelist Upton Sinclair, who ran a spirited but unsuccessful bid for the governorship of California in 1934, also increased public support for the idea.

The legislation that Roosevelt ultimately signed not only gave financial security to older Americans, it also provided a financial safety net for other vulnerable members of American society. It instituted programs of federal aid for the unemployed, children who lost family breadwinners to industrial accidents, and blind and crippled Americans. The money for these "social security" payments would be generated by new taxes on employers and the wages of working Americans.

Roosevelt and his administration of New Dealers recognized that the Social Security Act was a groundbreaking piece of legislation. For the first time in U.S. history, retirees and dependent children and disabled Americans would not be at the mercy of charitable organizations or other family mem-

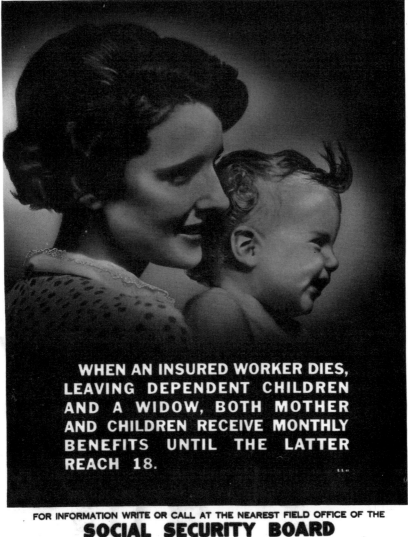

As part of its effort to encourage public enrollment in the new Social Security system, the Roosevelt administration printed posters such as this one highlighting various Social Security benefits.

bers (if they even existed or could help) for their survival. "This is truly legislation in the interest of the national welfare," stated Secretary of Labor Frances Perkins (see Perkins biography, p. 133). "It will make this great Republic a better and happier place in which to live—for us, our children, and our children's children. It is a profound and sacred satisfaction to have had some part in securing this great boon to the people of our country."[6]

Over time, Perkins's proud words have been borne out by the enduring success and popularity of the Social Security system. Enrollment started slowly, but by the 1940s most eligible people were in the program. Since that time, social security benefits have been fiercely protected by Democrats and Republicans alike. The system remains an integral part of the social fabric of twenty-first century America, protecting retired Americans and dependent children. Today, the Act is universally acknowledged by historians and ordinary Americans alike as the most enduring accomplishment of the New Deal era.

Labor Unrest Grows

The third major law to come out of the Second New Deal was the National Labor Relations Act of 1935 (also known as the Wagner Act in recognition of its leading author and sponsor, Democratic Senator Robert Wagner of New York). Growth in union membership in the United States had actually begun in 1933, when Roosevelt signed the National Industrial Recovery Act (NIRA). One part of this law—Section 7(a)—guaranteed labor the right to organize. This was extremely important to the union cause, which had floundered during the pro-business administrations of Calvin Coolidge and Herbert Hoover in the 1920s and early 1930s.

The passage of the NIRA gave labor activists and rank-and-file workers renewed confidence that they could band together and negotiate better wages and working conditions from their employers. Coal miners, textile workers, newspaper employees, dock workers, and numerous other workers rushed to join unions and strike for better pay and benefits. "Courage was contagious," according to the authors of one history of the era. "It multiplied by the industry and city, by the shop, by the county and the state…. It was good to release in triumphant mass action the long-pent-up bitterness, the helplessness, the defeats, the humiliations, not only of the depression but of the generations."[7]

By 1934, many unions had registered enormous jumps in membership. Membership in the International Ladies' Garment Workers' Union (ILGWU),

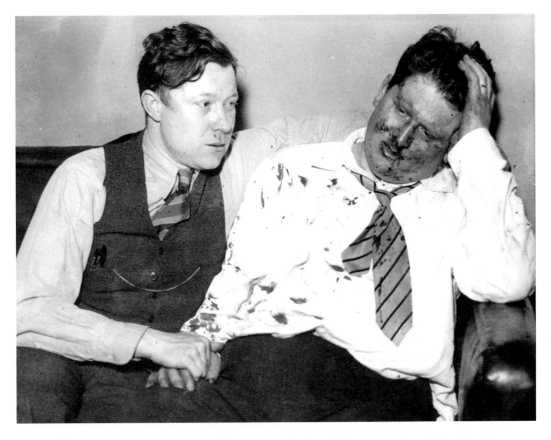

United Auto Workers' leader Walter Reuther (left) comforts fellow organizer Richard Frankensteen after they were attacked by Ford Motor Company thugs in the Battle of the Overpass.

for example, surged from 40,000 to over 200,000. The United Textile Workers Union (UTWU) saw its membership rolls explode from 20,000 to more than 340,000. But this growth did not always translate into wage hikes or better working conditions for members. Many companies tried to neutralize the unions by introducing their own company unions, which were easily controlled. Others simply refused to negotiate in good faith with union representatives, completely defying the provisions of the NIRA.

As a result, labor unrest rippled across numerous industries in 1934 and early 1935. Bitter and often violent strikes erupted at West Coast ports from Seattle to San Diego, in the textile mills of New England and the South, and in the coal fields of West Virginia and Pennsylvania. The unions waited anxiously for the Roosevelt administration to step in on their behalf. New Deal administrators, though, were reluctant to punish corporations. They did not want to further anger the nation's manufacturers and mining companies since they were so important to the administration's economic recovery plans.

In fact, some New Deal officials publicly condemned the labor movement's growing reliance on general strikes—actions in which unions from different industries struck together to pressure corporations into giving in to their demands. These types of strikes could paralyze entire cities, so they were viewed in the Roosevelt administration as enormously damaging to economic recovery. Hugh Johnson, the director of the National Recovery Administration (NRA), described general strikes at various times as "a menace to government," "ugly," and "a blow at the flag of our common country."[8]

The National Labor Relations Act

In May 1935 the NIRA was declared unconstitutional by the U.S. Supreme Court. This development angered Roosevelt, but it gave pro-labor lawmakers in Washington, D.C., an opening to put together a stronger law guaranteeing union rights. Wagner led the way in this effort. When Roosevelt signed the senator's National Labor Relations Act on July 5, unions gained more legal protection than they had ever enjoyed before. First, it gave labor unions new legal rights to organize and bargain with employers on behalf of their members. Second, it triggered a massive wave of labor unrest and union organizing that fundamentally changed labor-management relations in the United States for the next quarter-century.

The American labor movement took full advantage of the NLRA. The United Auto Workers (UAW), which had been founded only two months before as part of the larger American Federation of Labor (AFL), moved decisively after the new law was passed. It organized a series of sit-down strikes against General Motors, the world's largest automobile maker, in 1936 and 1937. These actions were so effective that General Motors was forced to recognize the union in February 1937. Other automakers like Chrysler and Packard quickly followed suit.

The Ford Motor Company was the industry's lone holdout. The company resorted to a ruthless campaign of violence, intimidation, and espionage to ward off the UAW. But incidents such as the so-called Battle of the Overpass, in which UAW legend Walter Reuther and other union officials were brutally beaten by company thugs, became a public relations nightmare for Ford. In 1941

Ford finally gave in and recognized the UAW. For the next two decades, the UAW negotiated labor agreements that lifted industry workers across the nation into the middle-class.

Other unions also registered important victories after the passage of the Wagner Act. Labor leaders such as Sidney Hillman (Amalgamated Clothing Workers of America), David Dubinsky (International Ladies' Garment Workers' Union), Charles Howard (International Typographical Union), and William Zebulon Foster (Trade Union Unity League) all played important roles during this period. But of all of the labor leaders of the 1930s, none possessed the power or influence of John L. Lewis.

Veteran labor leader John L. Lewis was the man most responsible for the 1935 creation of the Committee for Industrial Organization (CIO).

Lewis had first risen to prominence as the head of the United Mine Workers in the 1920s. But he became a true titan of labor in 1935, when he played a major role in the founding of the Committee for Industrial Organization (CIO). This coalition of industrial unions was initially part of the AFL, which was headed by William Green. But tensions over strategy and priorities prompted Lewis and the unions loyal to the CIO (including the UAW) to split from the AFL in 1936. Two years later, the CIO changed its name to the Congress of Industrial Organizations. By that time, it had already become the leading labor organization in the United States. Under Lewis's direction, it both advanced the cause of existing member unions and helped found important new unions such as the United Steelworkers of America (USWA) and the Communication Workers of America (CWA). At the end of 1937, the CIO claimed more than 6,000 local unions with a combined membership of over four million workers.

The AFL also remained a potent force, even after the departure of the CIO and its unions. It reported a total membership of 2.9 million workers at the end of 1937. The combined membership of the two labor organizations thus reached almost seven million workers—more than 18 percent of all non-farm workers in the entire United States. These numbers made the AFL and the CIO a formidable voting bloc in national politics.

Other Triumphs of the Second New Deal

As the 1936 president election approached, Roosevelt could point to numerous legislative accomplishments. He highlighted the policies and laws enacted during his First Hundred Days, as well as the jewels of the Second New Deal—the Social Security Act, the National Labor Relations Act, and the creation of the Works Progress Administration. In addition, Roosevelt trumpeted other victories of 1934-1935, such as the Public Utility Holding Company Act, which gradually dissolved most of the investment trusts that dominated private power production in the United States in the 1930s; the Banking Act, which overhauled the role of the Federal Reserve in monitoring the nation's banks; and the Rural Electrification Administration, which used loans to rural electric cooperatives to spread electricity to farmers, ranchers, and other residents of rural America.

> *"Roosevelt is rapidly becoming the most despised President in the history of the country," fumed one New Deal critic. "We're going to turn that cripple out of the White House.... He and his gang are in the death rattle."*

Another widely popular program from this period was the National Youth Administration (NYA), which provided part-time employment to students to help them pay for school and apprenticeships. Almost three million young Americans enrolled in this program during its existence. Of this total, nearly 300,000 were African Americans, thanks in large part to the tireless efforts of NYA administrator Mary McLeod Bethune. A dedicated civil rights advocate, Bethune was the highest-ranking African-American official of the entire New Deal era.

The NYA further increased African-American allegiance to Roosevelt. Black communities sometimes expressed frustration with Roosevelt's refusal to take a stand on many civil rights issues, but they nonetheless saw him as a friend. Agencies such as the NYA and the WPA helped millions of African-American families, and First Lady Eleanor Roosevelt repeatedly voiced support for black civil rights (see Eleanor Roosevelt biography, p. 137).

The 1936 Presidential Campaign

African-American voters were vital to Roosevelt's re-election hopes in 1936, for other voting blocs in America had become bitterly opposed to the New Deal president by that point. "Roosevelt is rapidly becoming the most

Support from farmers, working-class people, and African Americans enabled Roosevelt (second from right in car) to win a second term in 1936.

despised President in the history of the country," fumed Gerald L. K. Smith, a bigoted, nationally known minister, in a January 1936 speech. "We're going to turn that cripple out of the White House.... He and his gang are in the death rattle. We have only to put the cloth of the ballot over his dead mouth."[9]

The fiercest criticism of Roosevelt and his fellow New Dealers came from Republicans, conservative businessmen, and other citizens who feared that Roosevelt's policies posed a serious threat to the nation's future (see "The *Saturday Evening Post* Condemns Roosevelt and the New Deal," p. 197). They were joined by many influential newspapers that expressed fears that Roosevelt's New Deal programs gave too much power to the central government. "Businessmen and industrialists and their allies," observed one scholar, "looked at the various regulatory programs of the New Deal as the tactics of a government out to enslave business, stifle free enterprise, pander to the demands of radicals of all stripes, and give labor the power to dictate wages, hours, and other matters."[10] Or as one conservative critic put it, "The New Deal is nothing more or less than an effort sponsored by inexperienced sentimentalists and demagogues to take away from the thrifty what the thrifty or their ancestors have accumulated, or may accumulate, and to give it to others who have not earned it … and who never would have earned it and never will earn it."[11]

One of the most powerful anti-Roosevelt organizations was the American Liberty League. Formed in 1934, it was led by a coalition of wealthy conservatives from both the Democratic and Republican parties. Prominent members included John J. Raskob, owner of the Empire State Building; Alfred E. Smith, the 1928 Democratic presidential nominee; Alfred P. Sloan Jr., the head of General Motors; Howard Pew, director of Sun Oil; and the Du Pont family. These business and political leaders described the League as an association of freedom-loving Americans who believed that the federal government had no right to take hard-won personal wealth and give it to other individuals or groups. By mid-1936, the organization boasted more than 100,000 members, including a number of individuals who gave tens of thousands of dollars to the League to fight Roosevelt at the ballot box and in the courts.

Roosevelt and his allies regarded the League and other rich and powerful opponents as greedy millionaires who resented the loss of their near-dictatorial powers over American politics and commerce. Certainly, that is how Roosevelt tried to paint his opponents during the 1936 presidential campaign. "Powerful influences strive today to restore that kind of government with its doctrine that the government is best which is most indifferent," said Roosevelt at one campaign stop in New York City. "Never before have these forces been so united against one candidate as they stand today. They are unanimous in their hatred of me—and I welcome their hatred."[12]

In the end, the scorn of conservatives was not strong enough to defeat Roosevelt. In fact, the November election turned into a landslide victory for the New Dealer. Roosevelt enjoyed strong support from America's poor and working-class people—the main beneficiaries of the New Deal—and millions of other Americans who believed that the country needed to rein in big business and help the less fortunate (see "A Rabbi's Letter of Thanks to Roosevelt,"

Escaping Reality through Entertainment

One of the most contradictory phenomena of the Great Depression was the explosive growth of America's entertainment industry. Throughout this time of great economic misery and uncertainty, millions of Americans spent hard-earned dollars to buy movie tickets, attend jazz clubs, and purchase pulp magazines and "Big Little Books"—cheap, compact books that combined text and illustrations to tell the adventures of Dick Tracy, Little Orphan Annie, Buck Rogers, Tarzan, The Lone Ranger, and other children's heroes that were created during the 1920s and 1930s. By some estimates, 60 million Americans went to the movie theatre every week during the height of the Great Depression. Their patronage enabled the Hollywood-based film industry to become one of the few industries that actually grew during the 1930s.

The popularity of these various forms of entertainment has been attributed to two major factors. One factor was the low expense of indulging in these pastimes. Tickets for most movies, concerts, and theatrical productions were so cheap that all but the most poverty-stricken families felt that it was a cost that they could absorb. Similarly, individual copies of pulp magazines and Big Little Books only cost a few cents.

An even bigger factor, though, was the intense desire of Americans to escape—even if only for a few hours—from the grim news of the Depression. Movies such as *Gone with the Wind* and *The Wizard of Oz*, pulp magazines with titles like *Amazing Stories, Undercover Detective,* and *Famous Western,* and big bands led by Jazz legends like Benny Goodman, Duke Ellington, and Glenn Miller all gave Americans opportunities to forget the Depression for a little while and enjoy life again.

p. 202). Their votes lifted him to an easy triumph over Republican candidate Al Landon and the corporate interests who supported him. Roosevelt carried every state but Maine and Vermont, winning the electoral college by the largest margin ever (523 to 8). He also won the popular vote by more than ten million votes, claiming nearly 61 percent of all votes. In addition, the Democrats rode Roosevelt's popularity to increase their majorities in both houses of Congress.

Second-Term Struggles

Roosevelt and the Democrats took understandable pleasure in their historic victory in the 1936 elections. However, Roosevelt's second term as president began on a stormy note. First, he announced plans to reorganize the executive branch of the U.S. government to make its operations more efficient. This news alarmed some observers, who worried that Roosevelt was using the reorganization as a way to increase his power. These concerns were further heightened in February 1937, when Roosevelt announced a plan to "pack" the U.S. Supreme Court. He proposed to add a new justice for each sitting justice who, having served at least ten years, did not resign or retire within six months after reaching the age of seventy. Roosevelt stated that he would add no more than six additional justices to the court under this plan.

Roosevelt's motives for this proposal were clear to friend and foe alike. Throughout his first term, the conservative majority on the Court had been a thorn in his side. These justices had struck down major sections of his National Industrial Recovery Act in 1935 and blocked other proposed New Deal reforms as well. Roosevelt wanted to remove this obstacle by changing the make-up of the Court to one that would be friendlier to his administration's policies and goals.

This time, though, Roosevelt miscalculated the mood of the American people. They were greatly troubled by the emergence of dictatorships in Germany and Italy during the mid-1930s. So when Republicans charged that the president was acting like a power-hungry dictator, they listened. Roosevelt tried to reassure the citizenry, but his efforts did not erase their fears. Both his efforts to pack the Court and his bid to reorganize the executive branch failed to get the necessary support in Congress, even though his party controlled both houses.

Roosevelt's disappointment over the failure of his court-packing scheme was short-lived, though. Over the course of his second term, deaths and retirements on the Court enabled him to appoint five justices to fill vacant positions. The Supreme Court thus became much more liberal in the space of a few years, and it became a reliable defender of Roosevelt's New Deal policies and programs.

The "Roosevelt Recession"

In economic matters, Roosevelt's second term began on a much more optimistic note. The stock market was slowly regaining strength, and factories were churning out goods in ever-greater volumes. As factory production increased, unemployment figures also became more encouraging. Between August 1935 and May 1937, for example, factory employment in twenty-five major U.S. manufacturing industries jumped by almost 25 percent. Nationwide, the unemployment rate fell to 15.3 percent in December 1936—the lowest rate in six years.[13] Americans in many parts of the country expressed cautious optimism that the Great Depression was finally drawing to an end.

In the fall of 1937, though, the economy reversed course and fell into a slump that lasted for most of the following year. Most historians blame this so-called "Roosevelt recession" in part on Roosevelt's decision to cut funding for the WPA and other public works programs so as to balance the federal budget. This move reduced enrollment in the programs, which in turn lessened consumer spending. This reduction might not have been all that troublesome on its own, but even Americans who had more economic security remained cautious about spending their money. As a result, consumer buying failed to keep pace with the growth in production. When businesses realized that their inventories of goods were piling up, they put on the brakes at their factories. Industrial manufacturing production fell by one-third, industrial stock prices lost half their value, and nearly four million Americans lost their jobs.[14]

This downturn took a heavy toll on the morale of the American public. It also gave the Republican Party an opening to make gains in the 1938 Congressional elections. Republican candidates across the country claimed that the New Deal programs put together by Roosevelt and his Democratic colleagues were failures, and many Americans decided they were right. Republicans gained eight seats in the U.S. Senate and 81 seats in the House of Representatives in the November 1938 elections.

The changes in Congress made it harder for Roosevelt to carry out his legislative agenda and maintain existing New Deal programs. He did manage to convince Congress to pass the Fair Labor Standard Act of 1938, which established a minimum wage and set the work week at forty-four hours (later reduced to forty). But other victories were hard to come by. Congress slashed funding for the WPA's Federal Theatre Project, for example, and administration proposals to expand federal health care programs were derailed by Republicans and conservative southern Democrats.

These defeats frustrated many New Dealers in the administration. But Roosevelt barely reacted to some of the setbacks. By the late 1930s, his attention had became increasingly focused on Europe, where Adolf Hitler and Nazi Germany had emerged as an ominous threat to world peace.

Notes:

[1] Hansen, Ruth, interview with Kami Christensen, December 6, 1997, "Always Lend a Helping Hand: Sevier County Remembers the Great Depression." Available online at http://newdeal.feri.org.

[2] Quoted in Turkel, Studs. *Hard Times: An Oral History of the Great Depression.* New York: Pantheon, 1971, p. 86.

[3] Woodward, Ellen S. "The Lasting Values of the WPA," National Archives, *WPA Papers.* Available online at http://newdeal.feri.org/texts/499.htm.

[4] Howard, Donald S. *The W.P.A. and Federal Relief Policy.* New York: Russell Sage Foundation, 1943, pp. 125-28.

[5] Quoted in Sitkoff, Harvard. *A New Deal for Blacks: The Emergence of Civil Rights as a National Issue. Vol. 1: The Depression Years.* New York: Oxford University Press, p. 69.

[6] Perkins, Frances. "The Social Security Act," September 2, 1935. *Vital Speeches of the Day.* Pelham, NY: City News, 1935. Vol. 1, p. 794.

[7] Boyer, Richard O., and Herbert M. Morris. *Labor's Untold Story.* New York: United Electrical, Radio & Machine Workers of America, 1980, p. 291.

[8] Johnson, Hugh S. *The Blue Eagle from Egg to Earth.* Garden City, NY: Doubleday, 1935, p. 323.

[9] Quoted in Bennett, David H. *Demagogues in the Depression: American Radicals and the Union Party, 1932-1936.* New Brunswick, NJ: Rutgers University Press, p. 138.

[10] Watkins, T.H. *The Hungry Years: A Narrative History of the Great Depression in America.* New York: Owl Books, 2000, pp. 310-11.

[11] Quoted in Wolfskill, George. *The Revolt of the Conservatives: A History of the American Liberty League, 1934-1940.* Boston: Houghton Mifflin, 1962.

[12] Roosevelt, Franklin D. Address at Madison Square Garden, October 31, 1936. Available online at *The American Presidency Project,* http://www.presidency.ucsb.edu.

[13] Smiley, Gene. *Rethinking the Great Depression.* Chicago: Ivan R. Dee, 2002, p. 106.

[14] Polenberg, Richard. *The Era of Franklin D. Roosevelt, 1933-1945.* Boston: Bedford/St. Martins, 2000, p. 21.

Chapter Six

WARTIME PROSPERITY

—⊶⊷—

I have often said that there are no two fronts for America in
this war. There is only one front. There is one line of unity
which extends from the hearts of the people at home to the
men of our attacking forces in our farthest outposts. When
we speak of our total effort, we speak of the factory and the
field, and the mine as well as of the battleground—we speak
of the soldier and the civilian, the citizen and his Government.

—President Franklin D. Roosevelt, January 1944

The long economic nightmare of the Great Depression finally drew to a
close in the early 1940s. But the troubled years of mass unemployment, silent factories, and farm foreclosures were not defeated by Roosevelt's New Deal programs. Instead, it was World War II that ended the Great
Depression. U.S. factories roared to life to feed the surging demand for all
sorts of war materials, from tanks and fighter planes to uniforms and ban-
dages. Jobs became plentiful again—especially since the U.S. military
required so many men for the war effort—and American workers watched
with delight as their wages steadily rose. By the time the war ended in 1945,
many of Roosevelt's prized New Deal public work programs had been quietly
dismantled because they were no longer needed.

Turmoil in Europe

The Great Depression that afflicted the United States during the 1930s
also shook the rest of the world. In some places, economic problems became
so severe that they triggered political chaos and the rise of dictatorial regimes.
In Japan, military rulers took over the government and attacked China. In

Spain, a bloody civil war ended with the rise of a fascist dictatorship headed by another military leader, General Francisco Franco. And in Germany, Adolf Hitler and his Nazi Party completed their frightening rise to power, dramatically expanded German military strength, and initiated government-sponsored terrorism of Jewish citizens—all in the space of a few short years.

People in the United States watched these events unfold with rising concern. Speculation ran wild that the turmoil in Europe and Asia could trigger another world war. Most Americans wanted to avoid getting involved in any such conflict. They urged their elected leaders to steer them clear of this threat.

The tense situation in Europe exploded in September 1939, when Germany launched a swift and brutal military invasion of Poland. This episode marked the beginning of World War II. Hitler's armies then took over France, Belgium, the Netherlands, Norway, Denmark, Greece, and Yugoslavia in subsequent months. Nazi Germany's violent aggression brought several nations together to oppose Hitler. These Allied Powers included Great Britain, Australia, the Soviet Union, China, Canada, India, New Zealand, South Africa, Brazil, and other Latin American nations. But Germany's fearsome military machine did not stand alone. The armies of Japan, Italy, Rumania, Bulgaria, Hungary, and Finland all joined Germany's side in the conflict. These nations became collectively known as the Axis Powers.

At first, the United States took a neutral position in the war. Public opinion remained opposed to direct involvement in a conflict that was taking place thousands of miles away. But the war went so badly for the Allied Powers in 1940 that British Chancellor Winston Churchill and other Allied leaders repeatedly asked the United States for help. Many Americans supported such a move. They argued that it would be immoral to stand on the sidelines while the Nazis terrorized Europe. Others argued for intervention out of fear that Hitler might someday grow so strong that he could invade American soil.

Many other Americans, however, remained staunchly opposed to any involvement in the war. Around this time, a group called the America First Committee became the most influential opponent of American military intervention. The organization, which included some of the nation's wealthiest and most famous men, insisted that entering World War II would be disastrous for the United States. Members of America First included the famous aviator

Charles Lindbergh speaks at an America First rally in Cleveland, Ohio, in 1940.

Charles Lindbergh, longtime Democratic Senator Burton K. Wheeler, *Chicago Tribune* publisher Robert H. McCormick, and Robert E. Wood, the chairman of Sears, Roebuck & Co. "The America First Committee is a purely American organization formed to give voice to the hundred-odd million people in our country who oppose sending our soldiers to Europe again," said Lindbergh.

> Our objective is to make America impregnable at home, and to keep out of these wars across the sea.... It is not within our power in America today to win the war for England, even though we throw the entire resources of our nation into the conflict. With all our organization and industry, we are not, and will not be able to transport an army across the ocean, large enough to invade the continent of Europe successfully as long as strong European armies are there for its defense.[1]

Roosevelt Runs for a Third Term

For his part, Roosevelt maintained a policy of neutrality in 1939 and early 1940, when he announced that he would run for a third term as president later that fall. This announcement triggered a storm of criticism from Republicans, conservative business executives, newspaper editors, and even some people who had been reliable supporters of Roosevelt. At that time, there were no laws that actually prohibited Roosevelt from serving a third term. But throughout the history of the United States, an unwritten rule had established a two-term limit for presidents. Critics charged that by seeking a third term, Roosevelt ran the risk of turning the United States into a virtual monarchy—a government ruled by a king.

Roosevelt understood these complaints, but he was reluctant to turn over the reins of power at such a troubled time. After all, America remained in the grip of the Great Depression, and the war in Europe loomed over everything. In addition, many people told him that he had a responsibility to remain in the White House and guide the American ship of state through these turbulent waters. "Who other than himself was equipped by knowledge and experience to meet the challenges that would ... be made to the White House [during the next term]?" wrote one biographer. "It had been dinned into his ears for nearly two years now, by earnest voices for which he had great respect, that only he could supply the necessary leadership and that he was morally obliged to do so."[2]

Roosevelt's Republican challenger was Wendell Willkie, a corporate lawyer from Indiana who had never before held public office. Willkie focused much of his campaign criticism on Roosevelt's controversial decision to seek a third term. For his part, Roosevelt repeatedly assured the public that he would keep American forces out of World War II. But he also proposed to provide military and economic aid to the Allies, who were being routed by German forces across much of Europe. In addition, Roosevelt warned that the United States had to be prepared if the war somehow migrated over to American soil. He thus convinced Congress to pass the Selective Training and Service Act. This law, passed on September 16, 1940, authorized the conscription or drafting of 900,000 men for U.S. military service (this law was extended several times over the next few years, and the number of draftees eventually passed the 10 million mark).

Throughout this time, Roosevelt insisted that he would not let these military preparations interfere with his many New Deal reforms. "We must make

Roosevelt and the Twenty-Second Amendment

In 1797 George Washington, the first president of the United States, declined to seek election for a third term. He indicated that two four-year terms were probably the maximum that any one person should spend as president. Future presidents of the United States followed Washington's example, and American voters and lawmakers alike became accustomed to this tradition.

No formal law was ever passed establishing a limit of two terms for the presidency, however. So when Franklin D. Roosevelt decided to run for a third term in 1940, there was no law forbidding it. Roosevelt claimed that he ran for a third term because America needed an experienced hand in the White House to battle the twin threats of the Great Depression and World War II. Opponents claimed that he wanted a third term for more selfish reasons, but in the end the American public supported Roosevelt's bid. Four years later, American voters endorsed him for a fourth term as president.

Roosevelt died just a few weeks into his fourth term, though. After his death, Republican legislators led a campaign to pass a constitutional amendment that would limit a president to two four-year terms. The amendment was passed by Congress in 1947, and it was ratified by the states four years later. The Twenty-Second Amendment remains in force today, ensuring that Roosevelt will always be the only U.S. president ever to serve more than two terms.

sure ... that there be no breakdown or cancellation of any of the great social gains which we have made in these past years," he declared in a fireside chat to the nation on May 26, 1940. "There is nothing in our present emergency to justify a lowering of the standards of employment ... [or] a breaking down of old age pensions or of unemployment insurance. There is nothing in our present emergency to justify a retreat from any of our social objectives—from conservation of natural resources, assistance to agriculture, housing, and help to the under-privileged."[3]

On November 5, 1940—election day—the American people signaled their belief that Roosevelt was the man best equipped to deal with the many domes-

In 1940 and 1941, American shipyards such as this one roared back to life to provide military aid to Allied forces in Europe.

tic and international problems swirling around them. Willkie enjoyed strong support in rural parts of America, and he received endorsements from nearly four out of five newspapers across the country. But this was not enough to counter Roosevelt's strength in big cities with large working-class populations. Roosevelt received almost 55 percent of the popular vote and won 38 states. He earned a total of 449 electoral votes, compared to only 82 for Willkie.

The Arsenal of Democracy

After clinching a third term, Roosevelt focused on mobilizing American industry to help the Allies in Europe and improve U.S. defenses at home. "Thinking in terms of today and tomorrow, I made the direct statement to the American people that there is far less chance of the United States getting into war, if we do all we can now to support the nations defending themselves against attack by the Axis than if we acquiesce in their defeat, submit tamely to an Axis victory, and wait our turn to be the object of attack in another war later on," Roosevelt said. "We must be the great arsenal of democracy. For us this is an emergency as serious as war itself. We must apply ourselves to our task with the same resolution, the same sense of urgency, the same spirit of patriotism and sacrifice as we would show were we at war."[4]

In late 1940 and early 1941, the United States sent steadily larger shipments of military arms and other equipment to Great Britain. Shipments were later expanded to provide direct aid to other Allies as well, including the Soviet Union. Although these trends were denounced by America First and other U.S. isolationists who wanted nothing to do with the war in Europe, Roosevelt shrugged off their complaints.

Some companies were reluctant to convert their factories and other operations to the production of military equipment. Executives feared that if they made this switch before their competitors, they would lose valuable market share. But other industries that had been battered by the Depression made this transition gladly. The shipbuilding industry, for example, benefited immediately from the conversion to a "war economy." Aided by a New Deal agency called the U.S. Maritime Commission, American shipyards quickly shifted their operations to meet growing demand for supply ships, many of which were being lost to marauding German submarines. The U.S. shipbuilding industry had made only 71 ships between 1930 and 1935, but from 1938 to 1941 it built over 200 ships. These boats became essential to the U.S. effort to supply military, medical, and food supplies to Great Britain and other struggling Allied Powers.[5]

The Roosevelt administration also introduced measures to pay for its military build-up. In 1940 the U.S. government extended the income tax to virtually all Americans. From 1939 to 1945, the number of Americans paying federal taxes rose from 4 million to 43 million. But even though this tax increase flooded the U.S. treasury with new money, it still was not enough to cover the escalating cost of the war.

Roosevelt thus introduced war bonds that could be purchased by the American public. Buyers of these bonds received only modest interest on their investment. But war bonds were safe because the government guaranteed their value. This was an important consideration for Americans who still had vivid memories of the bank crisis of the early 1930s. In addition, many people felt it was their patriotic duty to buy them. Certainly, the war bonds provided the U.S. government with an important source of revenue. By the time the war ended in 1945, 85 million Americans had purchased more than $185 billion in war bonds.

America Enters the War

As the final months of 1941 ticked away, the United States remained unwilling to provide anything more than military and economic aid to the Allied cause. But that stand changed dramatically on December 7, 1941, when Japanese planes launched a surprise attack on the U.S. Naval base at Pearl Harbor, Hawaii. The stunning attack killed more than 2,300 Americans, wounded hundreds more, and turned most of the base's ships and planes into flaming ruins.

The success of the attack pleased Japan's military leadership. But it also brought the United States armed forces into World War II after two years on the sidelines. Condemning December 7 as a "day of infamy," Roosevelt and the U.S. Congress immediately declared war on Japan, Germany, and the other Axis nations. The American public, which had been profoundly shocked and angered by the Pearl Harbor attack, firmly supported this move. Over the next several weeks, U.S. Army, Navy, Air Force, and Marine forces began deploying into the European and Pacific theatres, the two main geographic zones of the war.

As U.S. military forces shipped out, the Roosevelt administration hurriedly expanded its efforts to mobilize American industry and workers for the

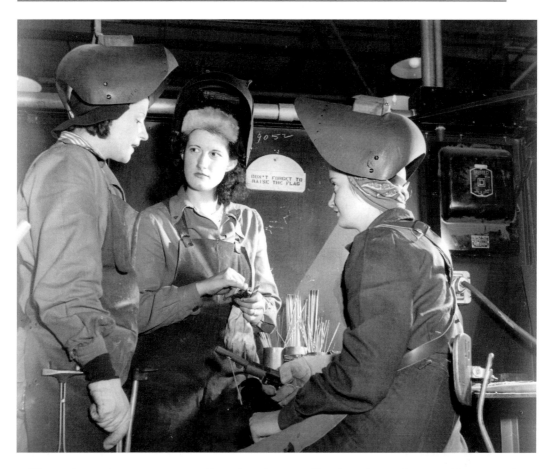

Millions of American women contributed to the war effort by taking jobs in a wide range of manufacturing industries.

war. It established numerous federal agencies that were responsible for making sure that industries produced the goods and equipment that the U.S. military would need. The most important of these agencies was the Office of War Mobilization, which was directed by James Byrne, a trusted advisor to Roosevelt and former Supreme Court Justice.

A Revitalized Economy

As millions of American men and women entered the military, industries of all shapes and sizes expanded their operations to meet the surging demand for everything from military clothing to naval aircraft carriers. Unemployment figures across the country shrank dramatically as factories added new shifts and trucking, shipping, aviation, and railroad companies scrambled to transport supplies to soldiers at domestic and overseas military bases.

By the time the war ended in 1945, it had created an estimated 17 million new jobs across America. Many of these jobs were taken by women. Since so many men were being called to fight in the war, companies added women to their payrolls like never before. Until this time, American society had severely limited the types of employment that women could seek. But during the war, homemakers, schoolteachers, secretaries, and seamstresses took jobs in aircraft manufacturing plants, munitions plants, and countless other factories generating war supplies. Their capable work in offices and on assembly lines across the country helped keep the war effort humming along. It also became an important early milestone in the quest of American women to gain greater career opportunities and workplace equality in U.S. business during the second half of the twentieth century.

As the war progressed, many U.S. companies returned to profitability. Workers shared in this bounty, in part because labor unions expanded in size and influence during the early 1940s. From 1941 to 1945, in fact, more than four million U.S. workers joined labor unions.[6] "World War II was the juggernaut that ran over American society," summarized one historian. "The war opened up for the first time for the majority of Americans the possibility of affluence rather than subsistence. For city dwellers, full employment and high wages offered the chance that, once private construction resumed after the war, they might be able to own their own homes and move to the suburbs. For farmers, war-time prosperity suggested that at the end of the war they might be able to enjoy the consumer goods—refrigeration, radios, and air conditioning—that rural electrification was making available to them."[7]

End of the New Deal

During this same period, Roosevelt's New Deal came to an end. To be sure, some New Deal policies and agencies lived on. Social Security, for example, grew to become the nation's most venerated federal program in the post-World War II era. Agencies like the Tennessee Valley Authority and the Rural Electrification Administration continued to do important work as well. But job creation had been the centerpiece of Roosevelt's New Deal programs, and in the early 1940s these programs became unnecessary. He thus phased out

Workers at a Long Beach, California, aircraft plant working on an A-20 attack bomber.

famous public works programs like the Civilian Conservation Corps and the Works Progress Administration.

Roosevelt also decided against supporting other reforms that would have further expanded the federal government's role in American business and society. He refused to endorse a bill that would have created a federal system of health insurance, for instance, and he approved a plan to set aside antitrust prosecutions of companies until the war was over. Roosevelt took these positions in part because he wanted to avoid wartime political fights with Republicans, who made gains in both houses of Congress in the 1942 midterm elections. But an even bigger factor was Roosevelt's focus on winning the war. "The war effort must come first and everything else must wait," he said.[8]

Roosevelt's focus on the war also led him to approve some policies and measures that were blatantly unconstitutional. For example, he approved a

A ship full of victorious American soldiers returning home at the end of World War II.

variety of measures to censor newspapers and private citizens that were critical of U.S. involvement in the war. Roosevelt's most controversial action of the war, though, came in February 1942, when he approved the forcible relocation of 110,000 Japanese Americans—two-thirds of whom were American citizens—into internment camps up and down the West Coast. This decision has been cited by many historians as the darkest stain on Roosevelt's entire presidency. "In time of peace, [Roosevelt] was genuinely committed to protecting individual liberty and freedom of expression," explained one scholar. "In time of war, however, he was prepared to impose harsh restrictions."[9]

Changing Tides of War

The entrance of the United States into World War II decisively changed the way the war unfolded—although it took a while for American military forces to really make their presence felt. For much of 1942, in fact, the Axis powers continued to make significant gains. German forces tightened their stranglehold over occupied territories in Europe, seized control of North Africa, and registered a string of decisive victories in the Soviet Union. Meanwhile, Japanese troops swarmed across Southeast Asia and the Pacific islands.

In 1943, though, the tide began to turn. American power guided Allied forces to important victories in both the European and Pacific theaters, and the German advance into Soviet territory was halted. Italy also switched sides in the war. The nation signed an armistice with Allied forces in September, after military dictator Benito Mussolini was overthrown.

The Allied forces registered a series of even more momentous victories in 1944. On the Eastern front of the European theatre, Soviet forces pushed the German army out of Soviet territory, then seized the Axis nations of Bulgaria, Romania, and Finland. To the west, a series of huge U.S. victories—like the June 6 "D-Day" invasion of Normandy, France, and the Battle of the Bulge at the end of the year—brought Nazi Germany to its knees. By early 1945 it was clear that Hitler and the German military machine he had created were on the verge of defeat. In February 1945 Roosevelt met with British Prime Minister Winston Churchill and Soviet Premier Joseph Stalin to discuss how they would treat Germany and other defeated Axis nations after the war was over.

A Legend Dies and a War Ends

Roosevelt did not live to see the war's end, however. In 1944 he had managed to win a fourth term as president, comfortably defeating Republican candidate Thomas E. Dewey. But he was dogged by poor health throughout the campaign season, and in 1945 his condition continued to worsen. Roosevelt died on April 12, 1945, of a cerebral hemorrhage. Vice President Harry S. Truman was quickly sworn in as America's thirty-third president.

Less than three weeks later, on April 30, Hitler committed suicide rather than face capture by approaching Soviet troops. Germany surrendered on May 8, ending the fighting in Europe. Japan refused to give up the fight for several months, but on August 6 and August 9, the United States dropped atomic bombs on the Japanese cities of Hiroshima and Nagasaki. The bombs destroyed both cities and convinced the Japanese military leadership that without atomic weaponry of their own they had no choice but to give up. They formally surrendered one month later, on September 2, 1945.

Notes:

1 Quoted in Berg, A. Scott. *Lindbergh.* New York: G.P. Putnam's Sons, 1998, p. 417.

2 Davis, Kenneth S. *FDR: Into the Storm,* 1937-1940. New York: Random House, 1993, p. 535.

3 Roosevelt, Franklin D. Fireside Chat, May 26, 1940. From *The American Presidency Project,* http://www.presidency.ucsb.edu.

4 Roosevelt, Franklin D. Fireside Chat, December 29, 1940. From *The American Presidency Project,* http://www.presidency.ucsb.edu.

5 Fischer, Gerald J. *A Statistical Summary of Shipbuilding under the U.S. Maritime Commission during World War II.* Washington DC: U.S. Maritimie Commission, no. 2, 1949, p. 41.

6 Blum, John M. V was for Victory: Politics and American Culture during World War II. New York: Harcourt Brace, 1976, p. 140.

7 Badger, Anthony J. *The New Deal: The Depression Years, 1933-1940.* Chicago: Ivan R. Dee, 2002, p. 310.

8 Polenberg, Richard. *War and Society: The United States, 1941-45.* Philadelphia: J.B. Lippincott, 1972, p. 78.

9 Polenberg, Richard. *The Era of Franklin D. Roosevelt, 1933-1945.* Boston: Bedford/St. Martins, 2000, p. 26.

Chapter Seven

LEGACY OF THE GREAT DEPRESSION AND THE NEW DEAL

⸺⁂⸺

He rises to an emergency as a trout to the fly. It is a test of his powers that he has never failed to welcome…. In Franklin Roosevelt there is fireman's blood, and he responds to the three-alarm bell like a veteran.

—Journalist Marquis W. Childs, 1940

By the time World War II ended in 1945, both the Great Depression and the New Deal had run their course. But the impact of the Depression, as well as Franklin D. Roosevelt's ambitious Depression-fighting program of economic and social reforms, continued to be felt all across the United States into the twenty-first century.

The New Deal—Success or Failure?

In the decades since World War II lifted American industry and commerce out of the Great Depression, many people have debated the legacy of Franklin D. Roosevelt and the New Deal programs he championed. Historians have pointed out that it was the war—not his policies—that ended the Depression. In addition, some conservative observers have been very critical of the ways in which federal power over U.S. business and commerce expanded under Roosevelt's watch. They charge that the New Deal trampled on the constitutional rights of business owners to operate their companies without government interference. They also claim that some of the social welfare programs implemented by Roosevelt created a cultural environment that placed less value on hard work and personal initiative. According to these critics, the New Deal gave the federal government too much influence over the lives of individual Americans—a problem that they feel still persists today.

Defenders of the New Deal acknowledge that the programs did not end the Depression. But they note that economic conditions *did* steadily improve through most of the 1930s. More importantly, the New Deal provided millions of Americans with the assistance they needed to weather the storms of the Great Depression until the United States could regain its economic footing. Without this help, millions of American families would have found themselves in much greater peril. Some scholars even believe that if the economic and social problems addressed by Roosevelt and his New Deal had been left untreated, the future of the United States itself might have been at risk.

Supporters of the New Deal also object to the notion that the government overstepped its boundaries during the Roosevelt years, or that it posed a threat to American capitalism. They claim instead that the New Deal reforms reflected the American people's desire for action, as well as Roosevelt's recognition that the foundations of the national economy needed major repair. "The overriding evidence in both word and deed," insisted one historian, "[was] that the Roosevelt administration came time after time to rescue capitalism and had no intention of replacing it."[1]

In fact, advocates assert that the New Deal showed future generations of political and community leaders that government had an important role to play in addressing social and economic problems. After all, several New Deal programs and policies remained in place long after the end of the Depression because of their popularity with the American people. These measures provided unemployment benefits, insured bank deposits, created easier paths to home ownership, protected stock market investments, dispensed pensions to elderly and disabled Americans, and ensured the right of unions to organize and bargain collectively. In sum, they gave ordinary Americans a safety net to keep them from plummeting into the worst depths of poverty and hopelessness.

All of these advances are now widely viewed as American institutions and integral threads in the nation's social fabric. Social Security, in fact, is now seen as a basic right of citizenship, and any lawmaker who dares to reduce the program's benefits risks political death. Most Americans now believe—as Roosevelt and his New Dealers did—that the federal government has a fundamental responsibility to safeguard the health and welfare of its citizens. As one historian wrote, "the New Deal, after all, reflected another deeply held belief with roots in the nation's pioneer past: that Americans take care of their own."[2]

Americans today view Social Security, which was established during the Great Depression, as a basic key to financial security in retirement.

Political Legacy of the New Deal

The Great Depression and the New Deal created a political coalition that dominated American politics for several decades—and which remained tremendously influential into the twenty-first century. The groups who bene- fited most from the New Deal included working-class people, farmers, elderly and disabled people, and union members. But perhaps no other group was lifted up by the New Deal as much as African Americans. Although their calls for increased civil rights went mostly unmet during the Roosevelt years, the president and his top lieutenants made special efforts to make sure that blacks could partake in the economic opportunities that were made available through the Tennessee Valley Authority, the Works Progress Administration, the Civilian Conservation Corps and many other Depression-era work pro- grams. As one scholar explained, "the idea of assisting the 'forgotten man' compelled New Dealers with a sense of shame and history to remember that

111

President Lyndon B. Johnson was able to pass his "Great Society" programs of the 1960s using the political coalition created by Roosevelt.

black Americans more routinely fell into that category than any other class."[3]

Memories of the helping hand they received from Roosevelt and other Democrats during the Depression kept all of these constituencies loyal to the Democratic Party for the next half-century. This coalition proved vital to the success of thousands of Democratic candidates running for office at the local, state, and national levels. "The coalition embraced southern whites as well as northern blacks, rural folks as well as urban immigrants, farmers as well as blue-collar workers, middle-class homeowners and jobless men and women," wrote one historian. "All [of them were] attracted by economic policies that benefited them and sometimes saved their lives, and by a recognition that the Democratic party, having introduced the welfare state, could be trusted to expand it."[4]

Time and again, the voting power of this coalition gave lawmakers the political muscle they needed to pass new laws and fund new programs for America's poor and working class. For example, Democratic President Lyndon B. Johnson would never have been able to pass his "Great Society" social programs in the 1960s were it not for the support of these groups. Collectively, these social welfare programs gave the federal government vast new authority over numerous aspects of American society and business. During Johnson's presidency, the United States passed landmark legislation in such areas as civil rights (the Civil Rights Act of 1964 and the Voting Rights Act of 1965), environmental protection (the Clean Air Act of 1963 and the Wilderness Act of 1964), education (the Elementary and Secondary Education Act of 1965), and health care (with the introduction of Medicare in 1965 and Medicaid in 1966).

This coalition remained mostly intact until the 1980s. At that time, however, the Republican Party effectively exposed major philosophical differences within the coalition itself. Union members, African Americans, and other tra-

New Deal-era public works such as Florida's Overseas Highway gave the United States a solid foundation for economic expansion in the post-World War II era.

ditional Democratic constituencies remained united on most economic issues. But they harbored very different feelings on a wide range of social issues, such as gun control and affirmative action. Politicians like Republican President Ronald Reagan capitalized on these differences to reduce the unity of the coalition. In fact, Reagan's ability to win two terms as president has been attributed by historians to his ability to attract traditional blue-collar Democratic voters to his side. These voters became known in the U.S. news media as "Reagan Democrats." Today, though, working-class people, African Americans, and other groups that united during the New Deal era are still more likely to describe themselves as Democrats rather than Republicans.

Economic Legacy of the Depression and New Deal

The New Deal stopped America's economy from sliding into outright ruin, and actually improved the nation's financial outlook in significant areas. By the time the United States entered World War II in 1941, employment levels, industrial production, and stock prices had all improved significantly

113

Could There Be Another Great Depression?

Since the end of the Great Depression, American historians, economists, lawmakers, and ordinary citizens have all debated whether another huge economic depression might someday hit the country. To be sure, the United States has experienced significant economic downturns since the 1930s. In fact, milder versions of depressions called recessions—defined as a decline in the national Gross Domestic Product (GDP) for two or more consecutive three-month periods—are fairly commonplace. According to the National Bureau of Economic Research (NBER), the country has fallen into economic recession eleven times from the end of World War II to the end of 2007. The most severe of these recessions took place from November 1973 to March 1975. But even this sixteen-month period of economic pain never expanded into a full-scale depression, which is usually defined as a GDP downturn of more than 10 percent.

The various financial and social institutions and programs that President Franklin D. Roosevelt created in the 1930s have been important factors in America's success in avoiding the economic misery of another full-blown depression. But some economists fear that existing trends in the United States place modern Americans at a greater risk of experiencing a depression than any generation since World War II. They cite statistics such as national home sales and home values, which declined more quickly in 2006-07 than at any time since the Great Depression.

from where they had been a decade earlier. Full recovery was reached in the mid-1940s, when the demand for war materials lifted numerous industries to new heights of profitability. And when the United States emerged from the war in 1945, the schools, parks, highways, airports, dams, sewer systems, and hospitals that had been created during the New Deal years gave the nation a strong foundation for explosive economic growth into the 1950s and beyond.

World War II caused other wide-reaching economic changes as well. For example, it re-established the United States as a consumer economy. Good-paying jobs became plentiful, giving families lots of spending money when the war ended. The war also changed the distribution of the U.S. population.

Not all economic indicators are cause for anxiety. On the positive side, unemployment rates in the United States remain at very low levels, and many Americans have ample financial resources to weather bad economic times. In addition, many large corporations are reaping annual profits that run into the billions (the richest of these companies—oil company Exxon Mobil—posted $40 billion in profits in 2007).

But other trends are more discouraging. American families have also accumulated record levels of debt; the average family owed $8,000 in credit card debt in 2007. In addition, millions of good-paying jobs have been sent overseas in recent decades, and the percentage of Americans living in poverty is on the rise. Also, many analysts worry that successful conservative campaigns to reduce government oversight of Wall Street has led to an explosion of greedy and irresponsible behavior by banks and other major financial institutions. All of these factors lead some analysts to worry that the housing crash may be an early sign of future economic turmoil.

Sources:

"A History of Recessions," September 4, 2007. Available online at www.cnbc.com /20510977.

Leonard, Andrew. "The Great Depression: The Sequel," April 2, 2008. Available online at www.salon.com/opinion/feature/2008/04/02/depression.

It prompted millions of Americans to relocate to the Atlantic, Pacific, and Gulf coasts, where many defense plants were located. Millions more migrated to Detroit, Pittsburgh, and other industrial centers in the Midwest. These population booms transformed affected regions into centers of explosive economic growth, for they generated huge surges in demand for housing, services, food, and other goods. These wartime migrations also accelerated the nation's turn away from rural life and farming livelihoods.

The postwar economic expansion was further aided by government policies and laws such as the Servicemen's Readjustment Act of 1944, better known as the GI Bill of Rights. This bill, which Roosevelt signed on June 22, provided a generous array of financial aid to returning veterans of World War II. It gave them tuition to attend college as well as other generous education benefits. The bill also provided veterans with federal loans to help them buy homes, farms, and businesses. About eight million veterans took advantage of this program in the first seven years of its existence—including millions of men and women who never would have been able to afford college otherwise.

The GI Bill has been widely credited as a key factor in the nation's amazing economic growth in the late 1940s and 1950s. It produced a new generation of engineers, educators, scientists, and technicians who played leading roles in developing important new scientific breakthroughs and technologies in the second half of the twentieth century. It also stimulated economic growth in housing, agriculture, and other industries, and it boosted the financial fortunes of colleges, universities, and vocational schools. Finally, the GI Bill had an important symbolic meaning to Americans. It reflected the idea—which was representative of the entire New Deal era—that all Americans who contributed to the nation's vitality deserved the respect and help of the government.

Another huge factor in America's economic resurgence after World War II was the shattered state of much of the rest of the world. The war had left much of Europe and large swaths of Southeast Asia in ruins, and the economies of these nations were slow to recover. The United States, whose railroads and factories and government offices never felt the impact of bombs or invading armies, filled this economic breach.

Roosevelt's Legacy

The Great Depression and the New Deal will always be closely associated with the man who led America during those turbulent years. And in most respects, Franklin D. Roosevelt is remembered fondly. In fact, surveys of historians routinely rank Roosevelt as the greatest U.S. president of the modern era. Moreover, these surveys almost always place him behind only the legendary Abraham Lincoln among the greatest presidents in the nation's entire history.

Roosevelt's enduring reputation is due in large measure to the role he played in changing fundamental aspects of American society. The role of the federal government in American life greatly expanded under his direction. In addition, American politics was forever changed by his ability to unite differ-

THEY (WHO) SEEK TO ESTABLISH
SYSTEMS OF GOVERNMENT BASED ON
THE REGIMENTATION OF ALL HUMAN
BEINGS BY A HANDFUL OF INDIVIDUAL
RULERS... CALL THIS A NEW ORDER.
IT IS NOT NEW AND IT IS NOT ORDER.

The Franklin D. Roosevelt Memorial in Washington, D.C., is dedicated to the memory of the president who guided the nation through both the Depression and World War II.

ent ethnic and cultural groups into a single potent voting bloc. Roosevelt also led the United States' emergence from isolationism to its present status as the world's leading military and economic power.

Another vitally important part of Roosevelt's rich legacy was his success in establishing the idea that American business had a moral obligation to respond to the needs of the larger society. Earlier presidents, such as Theodore Roosevelt (a distant cousin to Franklin), had made some progress in establishing the idea that big businesses should also be good citizens. But it was Franklin D. Roosevelt who firmly stamped this belief onto America society. As author Sherwood Anderson observed in the opening months of Roosevelt's years in the White House, the New Deal seems like "the death knell of the old idea that a man owning a factory office or store has a right to run it in his own way. There is at least an effort to relate it now to the whole thing, man's relations with his fellow men etc. Of course it is crude and there will be

117

no end of crookedness, objections, etc. but I do think an entire new principle in American life is being established."[5]

Finally, Roosevelt displayed an attitude of governance that became a model for future presidents and other political leaders. Whether delivering one of his trademark fireside chats or one of his four inaugural addresses, Roosevelt spoke reverently about the nation's past *and* confidently about its future. And unlike many other leaders of the time, Roosevelt seemed to believe what he was saying. As conservative writer George Will stated, Roosevelt "radiat[ed] an infectious zest" that enabled him to do "the most important thing a President can do: he gave the nation a hopeful, and hence creative, stance toward the future."[6]

Little wonder, then, that Roosevelt occupies such an exalted place in American history. By the time of his death in 1945, he had successfully steered the United States through the Depression, led the war effort that vanquished Hitler and Nazi Germany, and nurtured new programs and priorities that remain pillars of American society in the twenty-first century. "America, and indeed the world, differed markedly in 1945 from what it had been in 1933, to no small degree because of [his] actions," summarized one historian. "Roosevelt is one of the few American presidents who looms large not just in the history of the United States but also in the history of the world.... Franklin Delano Roosevelt continues to provide the standard by which every successor has been, and may well continue to be, measured."[7]

Notes:

[1] Rauchway, Eric. *The Great Depression and the New Deal.* New York: Oxford University Press, 2008, p. 106.

[2] Church, George. "Taking Care of Their Own: The New Deal Probed the Limits of Government," *Time,* March 9, 1998, p. 106.

[3] Rauchway, p. 107.

[4] Polenberg, p. 16.

[5] Quoted in Leuchtenburg, William E. *The FDR Years: On Roosevelt and His Legacy.* New York: Columbia University Press, 1995, pp. 244-45.

[6] Will, George. "The Splendid Legacy of FDR," *Newsweek,* February 1, 1982, p. 78.

[7] Leuchtenburg, William E. *The FDR Years: On Roosevelt and His Legacy.* New York: Columbia University Press, 1995, pp. 33-34.

BIOGRAPHIES

Herbert Hoover (1874-1964)

U.S. President during the Early Years of the Great Depression

Born into a Quaker family on August 10, 1874, Herbert Clark Hoover spent his early childhood in West Branch, Iowa. This community had been founded by his grandparents and other members of the Quaker faith, also known as the Religious Society of Friends. Both of "Bert" Hoover's parents died in the early 1880s, and at age nine, he went to live with relatives in Oregon, where his hours were taken up with school studies, farm chores, and work in his uncle's business. In 1891, he entered the newly opened Stanford University in Palo Alto, California. He graduated with a degree in geology four years later, at the age of 20.

The mining industry became Hoover's path to prosperity. After being hired as an engineer with an English firm, he was sent to Australia in 1897 to develop gold mines. His success there and in other international assignments led to a partnership in the company, and he later founded his own consulting business. By the time he reached his 40th birthday, he was a millionaire, and he and his wife, Lou, and their two children enjoyed a comfortable life in London. Hoover began to consider a role in public service, and when World War I broke out, he took charge of the Committee for the Relief of Belgium, which provided vital food supplies to civilians facing starvation because of the hostilities. After the United States entered the war, he was appointed as the nation's food administrator, and he also spearheaded postwar relief efforts in Europe.

Hoover's reputation as a hardworking problem-solver led many people to speculate that he had all the makings of a successful politician. Both the Republican and Democratic parties courted him, but he decided that the Republican Party was a better home for him. After an unsuccessful bid for the presidency in 1920, he served as secretary of commerce from 1921 until 1928 in the administrations of fellow Republicans Warren G. Harding and Calvin Coolidge.

During these years, Hoover displayed firm convictions about the course that his country should follow. Above all else, Hoover upheld the ideal of what he called "ordered liberty and the initiative of the individual." In regard to economic issues, he felt that most problems could be addressed through efficient organization and voluntary cooperation rather than bureaucratic programs and restrictions. He warned that strong state intervention would harm the creative innovation that had driven the country's success. This message was well-received within the Republican Party, which made Hoover its presidential nominee in 1928. In the November election, he easily defeated Democratic candidate Al Smith, carrying 40 states and 58 percent of the popular vote.

Grappling with the Depression

In October 1929 the U.S. stock market crashed in spectacular fashion. This crash exposed serious problems within the American economy and ushered in the Great Depression. The stock market crash shocked most people, but Hoover had privately expressed concern about unsustainable stock prices and speculative trading for several years. During the early months of his presidency, he had even urged Wall Street financiers to restrain their activities. But he took no decisive steps to regulate their practices. And when the crash came, he badly underestimated its impact. Hoover and many of his key advisors believed that the downturn was simply a necessary correction to an overvalued market, and they expected the economy to soon regain its momentum.

Shortly after the crash, Hoover called together leaders of industry and commerce and asked them to avoid cutting jobs and reducing wages. For a time, many businesses honored his request. Other initiatives followed, including a modest increase in public works projects, the creation of the President's Emergency Committee on Employment, and programs to stabilize food prices and loosen credit. These limited actions failed to stop the economy from spiraling downward.

Nevertheless, Hoover clung to his core belief in the soundness of the nation's economic system. He believed that the free market would recover on its own, and that large-scale government spending on works projects was unnecessary and unwise. He also rejected unemployment relief for those who lost their jobs. Hoover argued that such a program would undermine the ideals of self-sufficiency and personal initiative that were an essential part of the nation's identity, and he asserted that the most desperate people could be cared for by charitable organizations.

These positions created the impression among many Americans that Hoover lacked compassion for the downtrodden. In truth, the president spent most of his working hours studying the Depression, but he felt that his best course of action was to maintain an encouraging and upbeat public image. As the Depression deepened, however, his optimistic statements made him appear foolish to many Americans, who increasingly blamed him for the continued economic upheaval. His name was adopted for a wide range of developments associated with the Depression, from "Hooverville" shanty towns created by the homeless to "Hoovercarts"—automobiles converted to horse-drawn wagons because their owners could not afford gasoline.

As the grim effects of the Depression continued on into 1931, Hoover cautiously strayed from his policies of nonintervention. He convinced Congress to back a one-year moratorium on the debt payments owed to the United States by foreign governments. He believed that if these foreign nations received relief, they might buy more goods from Americans farmers and manufacturers. But the measure did not provide much help to American business. In January 1932 Hoover intervened in a more direct way than ever before. He worked with Congress to pass legislation creating the Reconstruction Finance Corporation (RFC). This agency provided government loans to banks and businesses and later offered funds for public works and work-relief projects. The RFC's initiatives were limited in scope, though, and they failed to halt the nation's economic slide.

Exiting the White House

By the presidential election year of 1932, nearly one quarter of the nation's workforce was unemployed. Yet Hoover stood by his principles and refused to provide direct benefits to the swelling numbers of destitute Americans. Instead, the Hoover administration actually raised taxes on most Americans in an effort to keep a balanced budget. The Revenue Act of 1932 doubled normal federal income tax rates for individuals and imposed new taxes on everything from gasoline to electricity. These new taxes angered millions of Americans who were already struggling to provide food, clothing, and shelter to their families. The president's popularity dropped even lower in the summer of 1932, when he ordered a harsh crackdown on a "Bonus Army" of impoverished military veterans who had marched on Washington, D.C. for financial relief. The crackdown was widely viewed as further proof of his callousness.

Later that year, American voters dealt Hoover a resounding defeat in his effort to seek another four-year term. Instead, they handed the country's reins over to Democratic candidate Franklin D. Roosevelt, who promised bold government action to end the Depression. Roosevelt won 42 states and claimed 57 percent of the popular vote. Because of high turnout, Roosevelt received seven million more votes than Hoover.

Not long after departing the White House, Hoover began to publicly criticize Roosevelt's New Deal economic reforms. He argued that his successor was creating "a planned society" that rejected individual freedom and punished entrepreneurial spirit. As the 1936 presidential election approached, he made an attempt to attain his party's nomination. But his fellow Republicans were unwilling to support a man who had been so soundly turned out of office four years before.

Hoover opposed American involvement in World War II until the December 1941 attack on Pearl Harbor by Japanese forces. As the war progressed he served as chairman of relief organizations for Poland, Finland, and Belgium. In 1947 President Harry S. Truman appointed him as chair of the Commission on Organization of the Executive Branch of the Government. This group, which came to be known as the Hoover Commission, made hundreds of recommendations to make the U.S. government more efficient. About three-fourths of them were eventually adopted. In the early 1950s Hoover headed up a similar commission, called the Commission on Government Operations.

In the late 1950s and early 1960s, Hoover spent much of his time writing. He published his memoirs as well as a study of President Woodrow Wilson. He also produced a multivolume work entitled *Freedom Betrayed* that attacked his nemesis Roosevelt and was said to include many sensational accusations, but it was never published. He passed away on October 20, 1964, at the age of 90.

Sources:

Fausold, Martin L. *The Presidency of Herbert C. Hoover*. Lawrence, KS.: University of Kansas Press, 1985.

Hamilton, David E. "War on a Thousand Fronts: Herbert Hoover and the Great Depression." In *Uncommon Americans: The Lives and Legacies of Herbert and Lou Henry Hoover*, edited by Timothy Walch. Westport, CT: Praeger, 2003.

Smith, Gene. *The Shattered Dream: Herbert Hoover and the Great Depression*. New York: Morrow, 1970.

Smith, Richard Norton. *An Uncommon Man: The Triumph of Herbert Hoover*. New York: Simon and Schuster, 1984.

Harry Lloyd Hopkins (1890-1946)
New Deal Administrator and Presidential Advisor

Harry Lloyd Hopkins was born on August 17, 1890, in Sioux City, Iowa. He spent his early years in a number of Midwestern towns, where his restless father pursued various business ventures. His mother was a greater childhood influence. A pious Methodist, she schooled her children in her religious faith and emphasized the importance of a good education. She eventually steered the family to a more settled existence in Grinnell, Iowa.

After completing high school, Hopkins enrolled at Grinnell College. During his time there he became heavily influenced by the social gospel movement, which called for activism and progressive reform in order to reshape society in accordance with Christian principles. This outlook helped steer Hopkins toward a career in social work. Immediately after his graduation in 1912, he moved to New York City and joined the staff of the Christodora Settlement House. One year later he married Ethel Gross, with whom he started a family. Hopkins then moved on to other charitable organizations and government agencies, including the Association for Improving the Condition of the Poor and the Board of Child Welfare in New York.

Working for Social Justice

During this period, Hopkins refined the ideas that would underlie his later career. Focusing on the problem of unemployment, he rejected the long-held notion that all unemployed Americans were simply lazy or incapable of working. Instead, he adopted a view—increasingly common among his colleagues—that business cycles in the economy heavily influenced unemployment trends. Hopkins also came to believe that it was the responsibility of government to help those who suffered from these economic downturns.

Over time, Hopkins developed distinct preferences about the form of assistance that government should provide. Rather than simply providing money or goods to those in need—what was commonly called "the dole"—he advocated work relief programs in which individuals performed tasks in government-created projects in exchange for wages. In a speech he delivered during his years as a federal administrator, he offered a simple summary of his views: "Give a man a dole and you save his body and destroy his spirit; give him a job and pay him an assured wage, and you save both body and spirit."[1]

Hopkins rose through the ranks at the American Red Cross, which he joined in 1917, to become a leading administrator. In 1922 he left the Red Cross to become the director of the New York Tuberculosis and Health Association (NYTHA). In both of these organizations, Hopkins demonstrated the qualities that would later make him such a valuable asset to the Roosevelt administration. A gifted leader, he inspired confidence in his subordinates and gave them the training and support they needed to accomplish their tasks. He was also a masterful organizer with a knack for redesigning organizations to make them more efficient.

Even as his professional career soared, though, Hopkins faced an unsettled personal life. Hopkins' expensive personal tastes—he was fond of fine restaurants, nightclubs, and wagering on horse races—often put him on the edge of financial peril. Turbulent romantic relationships also marked this part of his life. Hopkins's first marriage produced four children but ended in divorce in 1931. He wed Barbara Duncan later that year. They had one daughter together before her death from cancer in 1937. In 1942 he married a third time, to Louise Macy.

Director of the Works Progress Administration

It was the crisis of the Great Depression that brought Harry Hopkins together with Franklin D. Roosevelt, who was then the governor of New York. In 1931, Roosevelt chose Hopkins as the executive director of the state's newly created Temporary Emergency Relief Administration (TERA). This Depression-fighting agency provided relief to thousands of the state's most vulnerable citizens.

Following Roosevelt's election as president, Hopkins coauthored a plan for a national relief agency that was closely patterned after TERA. In May 1933 he was appointed director of the Federal Emergency Relief Administration, one of the first of Roosevelt's New Deal reform programs. Six months later, Hopkins was tapped by Roosevelt to direct the Civil Works Administration (CWA), a federal work program for the unemployed.

Hopkins made his biggest impact, however, as head of the Works Progress Administration (WPA). Founded in 1935, this New Deal agency quickly emerged as the centerpiece of the administration's work-relief efforts during the Great Depression. Under Hopkins's direction, the WPA created more than three million jobs a year for seven consecutive years. Critics condemned some WPA projects as poorly managed, frivolous "make-work" schemes that wasted billions of tax dollars. But Hopkins and other WPA administrators pointed out that the WPA built schools, hospitals, parks, bridges, and roadways all across the country. And even critics of the WPA acknowledged that Hopkins directed the agency with integrity.

When Hopkins had first arrived in Washington, D.C., in the early 1930s, he had hoped to stay out of political disputes. Over time, though, Hopkins came to accept them as part of his job. He became skilled at defending and promoting the actions of the WPA and other New Deal programs and agencies. He also proved himself a shrewd strategist in power struggles that took place within Roosevelt's inner circle.

By the late 1930s Hopkins had managed to position himself as a leading candidate to succeed Roosevelt, who was planning to leave office at the end of his second term. In December 1938 Roosevelt appointed Hopkins as secretary of commerce, a position that the administrator thought would further burnish his image in advance of the 1940 election. But severe health problems (including a bout with cancer), opposition from fellow New Dealers like Secretary of the Interior Harold Ickes, and questions about his careless spending habits all overshadowed his widely recognized concern for the poor. By the time Roosevelt decided to seek re-election to a third term instead of retiring, Hopkins's presidential aspirations had already faded.

Wartime Diplomat and Advisor

After Roosevelt's election to a third term in November 1940, Hopkins became a fixture at the White House. He and his daughter Diana took up residence there, and he became known as a member of the president's extended family. The close friendship between the two men further deepened during World War II. In 1940 and 1941, when German forces threatened to conquer all of Europe, Roosevelt gave Hopkins responsibility for overseeing America's Lend-Lease initiative, which provided arms and supplies to Great Britain, the Soviet Union, and other Allied nations. Following the Japanese attack on the

U.S. naval base at Pearl Harbor in December 1941, Hopkins's advice and oversight helped guide the president's war policy, and he played a pivotal role in bringing the American armed forces to a combat footing.

On the diplomatic front, Hopkins was a key intermediary who helped coordinate the actions of the United States and its allies. He frequently traveled to Europe to confer with figures such as British Prime Minister Winston Churchill and Soviet Premier Joseph Stalin. He also accompanied Roosevelt to all of the major wartime conferences. In addition, he helped lay the groundwork for the creation of the United Nations as the conflict moved toward its conclusion. An appreciative Churchill even went so far as to start referring to the plainspoken Hopkins as "Lord Root of the Matter." This view was shared by many other world leaders who admired the American's ability to forge a consensus on difficult issues.

Hopkins's achievements in World War II were all the more remarkable given his poor health. His medical difficulties had begun in the mid-1930s, when he was diagnosed with stomach cancer, and he later suffered from other digestive ailments that often left him malnourished. During the war years, his condition was frequently very grave. On one occasion, he had to be carried off his plane when it arrived in England, and by war's end it was clear that he did not have long to live. Despite his difficulties, though, he outlived Roosevelt and assisted President Truman in the early months of his administration. In July 1945, he left government and returned to New York, where he worked briefly as a mediator before being hospitalized. He passed away on January 29, 1946, at the age of 55.

Sources:

Adams, Henry H. *Harry Hopkins*. New York: G. P. Putnam's Sons, 1977.

Hopkins, June. *Harry Hopkins: Sudden Hero, Brash Reformer*. New York: St. Martin's, 1999.

McJimsey, George. *Harry Hopkins: Ally of the Poor and Defender of Democracy*. Cambridge, Mass.: Harvard University Press, 1987.

Sherwood, Robert E. *Roosevelt and Hopkins: An Intimate History*. New York: Enigma, 2001.

Notes:

[1] Quoted in Hopkins, June. *Harry Hopkins: Sudden Hero, Brash Reformer*. New York: St. Martin's, 1999, p. 164.

Hugh S. Johnson (1882-1942)
Director of the New Deal's National Recovery Administration

Hugh Samuel Johnson was born on August 5, 1882, in Fort Scott, Kansas. His childhood was marked by frequent moves, and he received an early lesson in economics when a downturn in the business cycle bankrupted his father's real estate enterprise. The family's fortunes improved in the mid-1890s when Hugh's father became the postmaster and a prominent political figure in the town of Alva, Oklahoma.

Thanks in part to his father's influence, Johnson entered the prestigious West Point Military Academy at age 17. He later described himself as a "a very bad cadet," but he managed to graduate in 1903. He wed Helen Kilbourne one year later, and they had a son together in 1907. Johnson's military career as a cavalry officer was undistinguished, but in 1914 he was offered the opportunity to attend law school and become part of the Judge Advocate Corps, which is the judicial arm of the U.S. Army (each branch of the armed services has a similar judicial arm). It was a big challenge, but Johnson responded with an astounding burst of energy and hard work. He completed the three-year course of legal study in half that time, graduating with honors.

The entrance of the United States into World War I proved another defining moment for Johnson. He helped write the Selective Service Act of 1917 that created a new military conscription system and then took a lead role in planning and executing the draft. In 1918, he was named the Army representative on the War Industries Board (WIB), where he helped foster cooperation between the government and private industry in order to supply the armed forces. His administrative skills were recognized with the Distinguished Service Medal and with promotions that made him a brigadier general. In 1919, though, Johnson opted to leave the Army to pursue a career in business. After working as a senior manager at the Moline Plow Company, he became an assistant to Bernard M. Baruch, a well-known stock market speculator and political operative who wielded considerable power in the Democratic Party.

Joining the New Deal

Johnson's career as one of the nation's most famous New Dealers began in late 1932. During that time, president-elect Roosevelt was turning far and wide for advice and suggestions for attacking the Great Depression, which had settled like a dark cloud over the nation over the previous three years. Johnson's experiences with the War Industries Board, combined with his years in business, led Roosevelt's advisors to seek him out. Within weeks of Roosevelt's inauguration, Johnson was reviewing all sorts of legislative proposals to revitalize American business and industry on behalf of the White House.

In April 1933 Johnson reported that if the United States wanted to get back on the road to economic recovery, it should give Roosevelt wide authority to enforce new regulations on competition and labor practices.

That same month, Johnson joined with other experts to craft a plan to revive the nation's industries. The outcome was the National Industrial Recovery Act (NIRA), which became law in June 1933. To oversee the bill's broad agenda for stimulating business and improving pay and working conditions, the National Recovery Administration (NRA) was established, and Roosevelt appointed Johnson as its director.

The president's decision was based on his belief that the NRA needed a strong-willed leader. Johnson certainly met that standard, but his drive and focus sometimes made him impulsive and led to erratic behavior. More ominously, he had shown a previous history of combative behavior and drunken binges during times of stress. Concerns about Johnson's suitability as director of NRA surfaced even before he officially began his duties. Even his business mentor Baruch cautioned the president that Johnson was unstable. Roosevelt opted to stick with his choice, though he did remove the public works aspect of NIRA from Johnson's control at the outset.

Even with reduced responsibilities, Johnson faced an enormous task, but he set to work with the single-minded dedication that he had shown throughout his career. His first priority was to oversee the creation of codes of fair competition for the nation's leading industries. The process led to some startling developments, including the abolishment of child labor in textile mills and agreements on minimum wages, collective bargaining, and maximum work hours in a range of industries. In his eagerness to get executives to adopt codes of operation, though, Johnson often made major concessions to business leaders. In some cases he even abandoned provisions that had been mandated by the NIRA. And the talks with executives in steel, lumber, petro-leum, automaking, and other major industries went very slowly. "The codes did emerge one by one," said one historian, "but only after weeks of protract-ed and sometimes agonizingly difficult … negotiations that often had John-son hopping on airplanes and flying from one participant to another."[1]

As Johnson worked on these industry codes, he also took a leading role in introducing the "Blue Eagle" to American businesses and consumers. The Blue Eagle insignia was given to companies that agreed to obey the NRA's industrial codes of behavior. Participants could display this symbol on their products and throughout their stores—and thus show consumers that they were doing their patriotic part to lift the nation out of recession. Johnson launched a massive publicity campaign to spur public support for companies that cooperated with the NRA. Johnson himself was at the forefront, traveling city to city by airplane to deliver speeches that were littered with his gruff and colorful phrases that portrayed opponents as "chiselers," "rink-stinks," and "corporals of disaster."

These promotional activities played a big part in building public confi-dence in the early months of the Roosevelt administration. They also made Johnson famous. In the pivotal first year of the New Deal, Johnson and the National Recovery Administration were constantly in the news, and *Time* magazine even chose him as the magazine's "Man of the Year" for 1933.

The Falling Star

Even as Johnson became the most famous of Roosevelt's early New Deal-ers, his performance declined. His drinking intensified under the pressure of the job, and on more than one occasion he was visibly intoxicated in public. During this same period, the atmosphere at the NRA offices became increasing-ly confused and chaotic. Johnson became ever more reliant on his secretary, Frances "Robbie" Robinson, to organize his activities. But this arrangement became a source of controversy as well. Robinson was widely believed to be Johnson's mistress, so many people objected as her influence—and salary—rapidly increased.

By the beginning of 1934, the NRA was mired in a host of problems. Observers condemned the agency for its disputes with other government agencies, its inability to enforce compliance with industry codes, and its fee-ble attempts to control prices and settle labor-management disputes. In addition, public support for the agency quickly eroded as lavish promises of economic recovery failed to materialize. This greatly alarmed the Roosevelt administration, since the NRA was one of the most visible of all the New Deal programs. If people lost faith in the NRA, they might lose faith in other parts of the New Deal, too.

By the time Johnson reached his one-year anniversary with the NRA, many of his colleagues in the administration were seeking to remove him from his job. After months of deliberation, Roosevelt agreed. In September 1934, he accepted Johnson's resignation. Eight months later, the troubled NRA was laid to rest by the Supreme Court, which declared that large sections of the 1933 legislation that created the agency were unconstitutional.

Following his resignation, Johnson worked briefly with the Works Progress Administration in New York City before moving on to become a newspaper columnist and radio commentator. In 1935 he emerged as a harsh critic of the Roosevelt administration, which led to a bitter break with the president. In 1941 Roosevelt took his revenge by refusing to renew Johnson's largely symbolic commission in the Officers' Reserve Corps, thereby forcing him to give up the official title of "general." Johnson was deeply upset by the slight. Kidney and liver ailments forced his hospitalization later that year, and he passed away on April 14, 1942.

Sources:

Johnson, Hugh. *The Blue Eagle from Egg to Earth*. New York: Greenwood, 1968.

Ohl, John Kennedy. *Hugh S. Johnson and the New Deal*. Dekalb, IL: Northern Illinois University Press, 1983.

Watkins, T.H. *The Hungry Years: A Narrative History of the Great Depression in America*. New York: Owl Books, 2000.

Notes:

[1] Watkins, T.H. *The Hungry Years: A Narrative History of the Great Depression in America*. New York: Owl Books, 2000, p. 196.

Frances Perkins (1880-1965)
Progressive Activist and Secretary of Labor
during the Great Depression

Fannie Coralie Perkins (who adopted the name of "Frances" as an adult) was born in Boston, Massachusetts, on April 10, 1880. She grew up in Worcester, Massachusetts, in a prosperous family that encouraged her to pursue her education. As a student at the all-female Mount Holyoke College, she displayed both an impressive intellect and natural leadership abilities; she was elected president of her 1902 graduating class. That same year, she attended a campus lecture by Florence Kelley, the secretary of the National Consumers League. The league was a progressive organization devoted to improving working conditions for industrial laborers, and Kelley's presentation inspired Perkins to pursue a career in the field of social work.

After graduation Perkins went to Chicago, where she worked as a teacher and social worker. In 1909 she moved to New York City to conduct research on slum conditions for the New York School of Philanthropy and to complete graduate studies at Columbia University. Shortly after celebrating her 30th birthday in 1910, she found herself working alongside her role model, Florence Kelley, after being hired as the secretary of the New York City Consumers League.

Advocate for Workplace Reform

Devoting herself to the organization's legislative lobbying efforts, Perkins scored a major victory in 1912 when she helped obtain passage of the so-called 54-Hour Bill. This legislation placed new limits on the working hours of women and children in the state of New York. She also established herself as an authority on hazardous workplace conditions in unregulated factories and other businesses. The danger of some of these factories became tragically clear on the afternoon of March 25, 1911, when the Triangle Waist Company, a garment factory in Manhattan, went up in flames, killing more than 140 people. Perkins was among the horrified onlookers who watched workers leap from the windows of the blazing building to escape the flames.

After the Triangle tragedy, a group of concerned citizens formed the Committee on Safety of the City of New York, and Perkins was named its executive secretary. In that capacity, she became deeply involved in the work of the New York State Factory Investigating Commission, which conducted one of the nation's most thorough studies of occupational conditions. Its findings led to the passage of 36 new statutes, and Perkins later commented that "I wrote with [my] own hands most of the New York State labor law that was finally passed."[1]

Perkins's personal life during this time was turbulent. She married Paul C. Wilson in 1913, though she opted to retain her own name because of her feminist beliefs. After giving birth to a daughter in 1916, she intended to focus on her family. In 1918, however, her husband showed increased signs of mental illness (he spent the rest of his life in and out of mental institutions). Wilson's health problems forced Perkins to return to full-time employment to provide for her family.

Joining the Cabinet

In 1918 Perkins was named to the New York State Industrial Commission. She served on the commission for most of the 1920s, but in 1929 she was promoted to industrial commissioner by New York Governor Franklin D. Roosevelt. Perkins also took a leading role in overseeing the relief programs that Roosevelt organized across the state after the Great Depression struck in 1929.

By the time that Roosevelt decided to run for president in 1932, Perkins had become one of his most valuable and trusted lieutenants. She helped him hone the economic message that was at the heart of his campaign, and when he won the presidential election in November 1932, she was frequently mentioned as a candidate for a cabinet post in the Roosevelt administration. The speculation proved true, for Roosevelt offered her the position of secretary of labor. "I had more sense of obligation to [accept the nomination] for the sake of other women than I did for any other one thing," she said.[2]

Perkins wasted little time in making her presence felt in the Roosevelt administration. Within a few weeks, she unveiled an ambitious slate of programs addressing everything from public works proposals to unemployment relief and new wage and hour regulations. Many of these proposals would become centerpieces of Roosevelt's so-called New Deal social reform initiatives.

Over the next few years, Perkins helped shepherd many of these proposals into law. In many cases, she served as an arbitrator who created unified plans from the swirl of competing proposals generated by Roosevelt's advisors. She was especially important in shaping and passing important New Deal reforms such as the 1933 National Industrial Recovery Act (NIRA), the 1935 Social Security Act, and the 1938 Fair Labor Standards Act. Perkins was proud of her work on all of these laws, but she was especially thrilled by the passage of the Social Security Act. She proclaimed it to be one of the wisest and most compassionate acts of legislation ever to be passed in the United States.

Labor Unrest and Controversy

As labor secretary throughout the Great Depression, Perkins became personally involved in many of the strikes and labor disturbances that took place during the 1930s. In most of these labor-management disputes, she remained resolutely neutral. She also opposed using federal and state troops to break up strikes because she felt that such a move would signal support for management—and possibly trigger violence. In 1934, for example, she refused to order troops into San Francisco to end a general strike called by city unions. She maintained a similar stance during the famous 1936-1937 sit-down strike by workers at General Motors in Flint, Michigan. Throughout this tense period, Perkins refused to condemn the work stoppage or the United Auto Workers leadership. Instead, she patiently promoted a negotiated settlement between the strikers and management.

Perkins's moderate stance made her deeply unpopular with some conservatives. These critics—who also loathed Roosevelt and the New Deal programs he championed—accused Perkins of being sympathetic to radicals who were determined to destroy America's economic system. These criticisms reached their peak in the late 1930s, when a labor organizer named Harry Bridges, who was not a U.S. citizen, was accused of being a Communist. Many people wanted Bridges to be deported immediately. Perkins, who oversaw the Immigration Service as part of her duties, ignored these heated demands. Instead, she followed the standard legal and judicial procedures in the matter and refused to rush to judgement on the deportation. Her stance drew the wrath of members of the House Un-American Activities Committee, who threatened Perkins with impeachment on the charge that she was obstructing justice. She was quickly vindicated in Judicial Committee hearings, however (the case against Bridges also fell apart around this time, though he would battle the U.S. government in court on multiple occasions over the next few decades).

Nonetheless, rumors and smear campaigns continued to focus on Perkins. Opponents often claimed that she was a Communist. Others sought to take advantage of deep levels of anti-Semitism in some parts of the country by charging that she was actually a Jew who had been born in Russia. Perkins calmly recited evidence that she had been born in the United States, and she declared at one point that "if I were a Jew, I would make no secret of it." Defenders also insisted that critics distorted her record. They observed that although Perkins championed many progressive reforms for workers, she often publicly disagreed with organized labor leaders on various subjects. She even opposed the 1935 National Labor Relations Act—a huge milestone in the advance of labor rights—on the grounds that some of its provisions were unfair to business.

By the late 1930s, Perkins had grown weary of the nasty political fighting and long hours of work that her position required. She expressed a desire to leave her post at the end of Roosevelt's second and third terms, but in both cases, the president convinced her to stay on. She did not leave the Department of Labor until May 1945, a few months after Roosevelt's death. The following year, President Harry S. Truman appointed her to the Civil Service Commission, where she served for seven years.

In 1952 Perkins's husband passed away. A short time later she returned to her first occupation—teaching. She became a visiting professor at Cornell University and later came to reside on the campus. Perkins continued her classroom activities until just weeks before her death on May 14, 1965, at the age of 85.

Sources:

Martin, George. *Madam Secretary, Frances Perkins*. Boston: Houghton Mifflin, 1976.

Mohr, Lillian Holman. *Frances Perkins: "That Woman in FDR's Cabinet!"* Croton-on-Hudson, N.Y.: North River Press, 1979.

Pasachoff, Naomi. *Frances Perkins: Champion of the New Deal*. New York: Oxford University Press, 1999.

Severn, Bill. *Frances Perkins: A Member of the Cabinet*. New York: Hawthorn, 1976.

Notes:

[1] Quoted in Pasachoff, Naomi. *Frances Perkins: Champion of the New Deal*. New York: Oxford University Press, 1999, p. 34.

[2] Quoted in Pasachoff, p. 73.

Eleanor Roosevelt (1884-1962)
First Lady of the United States of America during the Great Depression

Born on October 11, 1884, in New York City, Eleanor Roosevelt was a member of one of the nation's most wealthy and prominent families. One of her uncles, Theodore "Teddy" Roosevelt, even served as the 26th president of the United States from 1901 to 1909. Her early childhood, though, was marred by her father's alcoholism and her parents' marital problems. She also felt unattractive and boring compared to her glamorous mother.

Both of Eleanor's parents died before she turned 10, so she was raised from that point on by her maternal grandmother. "I was a solemn child without beauty," she later wrote. "I seemed like a little old woman entirely lacking in the spontaneous joy and mirth of youth." Events took a turn for the better after she enrolled at a girls' school in England at age 14, however. She thrived in this setting, and developed a strong sense of social justice and other liberal views under the guidance of staff mentors.

Building on what she had learned abroad, Eleanor returned to New York in 1902 and undertook volunteer work with several progressive social organizations. Her activism came to a halt after 1905, when she married Franklin D. Roosevelt, a distant cousin. Their first child was born the following year, and five more followed, including one who died in infancy. For a decade, Eleanor held to the traditional role of an upper-class wife and mother, but she did not find great fulfillment in her family life and yielded many of her parenting duties to her strong-willed mother-in-law. Her husband, meanwhile, embarked on the beginning of his long and successful career in politics.

With the nation's entrance into World War I, Eleanor Roosevelt once more took up volunteer work, but it was a personal crisis that had a greater effect on her destiny. In 1918 she discovered that her husband was engaged in an extramarital affair. After considering divorce, the couple decided to remain together, but the painful episode inspired Eleanor to pursue a greater degree of independence. From that point forward, the couple forged a unique partnership that continued through their time in the White House. On the one hand, Roosevelt advised her husband on a variety of issues and supported him in many ways, particularly after he contracted the dreaded disease polio in 1921. But she also devoted time to her own projects, interests, and causes, including work with progressive organizations such as the National Consumers League and the Women's Trade Union League. Franklin and Eleanor's separate spheres were underlined by their living arrangements. Eleanor spent much of her time at her own home in Hyde Park, New York, while her husband lived and worked in New York City and the state capital of Albany.

A New Kind of First Lady

When Franklin was inaugurated as president in early 1933, Eleanor immediately redefined the role of first lady. She supervised many of the day-to-day domestic operations inside the White House, as many of her predecessors had done. But unlike other first ladies, she also became a forceful figure in her husband's administration in terms of shaping policy and responding to important events.

Throughout the Roosevelt presidency, Eleanor was a trusted advisor and dedicated advocate for numerous social causes, from relief for the poor to expanded civil rights for African Americans. This arrangement led some critics to portray Franklin as a hen-pecked chief executive. But he welcomed the exchange of ideas with his wife, especially in the early years of his presidency, and used it as a means to firm up the positions he took publicly. "Say what you think," he told his wife on one occasion. "If you get me in Dutch, I'll manage to get myself out. Anyway, the whole world knows I can't control you."[1] It was a message she took to heart, and she occasionally challenged her husband's policies in public. There were limits to her influence, but her power was well understood by prominent figures in the administration, who actively sought her advice and support.

Eleanor Roosevelt also presented her opinions directly to the public. Shortly after entering the White House, she began holding weekly press conferences that were restricted to female reporters—a tactic that allowed her to not only promote her views but also to encourage newspapers to hire women journalists. In 1935, she began writing a daily column, "My Day," that appeared in papers around the country, and she wrote several books and frequently spoke on the radio and in public lectures. In addition, she regularly traveled the country to help focus attention on various problems or programs. All of these activities made her, in the words of political columnist Raymond Clapper, "a Cabinet minister without portfolio—the most influential woman of our times."

Throughout the Great Depression, Roosevelt supported causes that benefited those she felt were most in need of help. She enthusiastically backed the administration's work-relief and pro-labor measures and frequently brought her influence to bear in helping specific groups, including rural residents of Appalachia and garment workers of the northern cities. The issue of women's rights was perhaps closest to her heart. Anticipating a change that would become increasingly common in the following decades, she voiced her belief that women should work outside the home and that no woman should be denied the opportunity to "do something which expresses her own personality even though she may be a wife and mother."[2] On a practical level, she joined with other prominent activists in an effort to bring more women into government service and also succeeded in her efforts to give women a larger voice in the Democratic Party.

The first lady was also a pioneer in the area of civil rights. Roosevelt focused significant attention on race discrimination at a time when few political leaders were willing to confront the issue. In addition to lobbying for federal anti-lynching legislation seeking greater equality in the armed forces during World War II, she refused to observe segregated seating arrangements and other forms of discrimination during her travels. "We must learn to work together, all of us, regardless of race or creed or color," she stated in a 1934 speech. "We go ahead together or we go down together."[3] She was also sympathetic to the difficulties faced by young people in the Depression and offered guidance to the leaders of American Youth Congress, despite the fact that some of the group's members were radical leftists.

Such positions invited a great deal of criticism from conservative opponents of the Roosevelt White House. Some detractors even leveled false charges that she was a Communist and an enemy of Catholicism and other Christian religions. FBI director J. Edgar Hoover closely monitored her activities for decades in the belief that she was a potential security risk.

Nonetheless, Eleanor Roosevelt's support for the causes she believed in never wavered. Her influence helped carry forth many of the New Deal's progressive initiatives, and she greatly influenced public opinion on issues that would become increasingly important in later decades. Roosevelt understood her role as an agent of change and embraced it, declaring that "there is nothing so exciting as creating a new social order."[4] Her compassion and independence also made her enormously popular with most Americans.

First Lady to the World

Mrs. Roosevelt remained a prominent figure during World War II. But the president became less welcoming of her opinions and criticisms during this period, and their lives became even more divided. "He might have been happier with a wife who had been completely uncritical," she noted after Roosevelt's death in early 1945. "Nevertheless, I think that I sometimes acted as a spur, even though the spurring was not always wanted nor welcome. I was one of those who served his purposes."[5]

Eleanor Roosevelt's engagement with the major issues of her time did not diminish after she departed the White House in April 1945. Later that year, President Truman appointed her as a U.S. delegate to the United Nations General Assembly, and she later became chair of the U.N. Committee on Human Rights and was one of the primary shapers of the body's Universal Declaration of Human Rights. This work and her international travels made her an admired figure around the globe and earned her the nickname of "first lady to the world." She remained a prominent figure in Democratic politics and worked diligently to maintain the values and policies of the New Deal in the post-war era while also promoting civil rights and a wide range of other issues. After John F. Kennedy was elected president, he appointed Eleanor Roosevelt to several official posts, and in the final year of her life, she chaired the President's Commission on the Status of Women. She passed away on November 7, 1962, at the age of 78 as a result of bone marrow tuberculosis.

Sources:

Cook, Blanche Wiesen. *Eleanor Roosevelt.* 2 vols. New York: Viking, 1992, 1999.

Hoff Wilson, Joan, and Majorie Lightman, eds. *Without Precedent: The Life and Career of Eleanor Roosevelt.* Bloomington: Indiana University Press, 1984.

Roosevelt, Eleanor. *The Autobiography of Eleanor Roosevelt.* 1961. Cambridge, MA: Da Capo Press, 2000.

Notes:

[1] Quoted in Cook, Blanche Wiesen. *Eleanor Roosevelt: Vol. 2, The Defining Years, 1933-1938.* New York: Penguin, 2000, p. 37.

2 Quoted in Cook, p. 74.
3 Quoted in Cook, p. 185.
4 Quoted in Cook, p. 618.
5 Roosevelt, Eleanor. *The Autobiography of Eleanor Roosevelt.* 1961. Cambridge, MA: Da Capo Press, 2000, p. 279.

Franklin D. Roosevelt (1882-1945)
U.S. President during the Later Years of the Great Depression and World War II

Franklin Delano Roosevelt was born on January 20, 1882, in Hyde Park, a wealthy community that sits on the shore of the Hudson River in New York State. His father was James Roosevelt, a successful railroad business executive, and his mother was Sara Delano. Both parents came from families of wealth and privilege, so young Franklin benefited from educational and travel opportunities that were not available to most boys. He attended the finest schools and received instruction from private tutors, and he frequently traveled with his family to Europe and other exotic destinations. His mother was an overprotective, controlling presence throughout these years, but Roosevelt nonetheless grew into a self-confident and independent-minded young man.

In 1900 Roosevelt enrolled at Harvard University, where he became editor of the school newspaper. He also established a romantic relationship at Harvard with his cousin Eleanor Roosevelt (niece of Theodore Roosevelt, who was president of the United States at the time). Franklin graduated from Harvard in 1904, and he married Eleanor one year later over his mother's objections. In 1906, when they had the first of five children, Roosevelt resumed his education at Columbia Law School. After two years at Columbia he passed the New York state bar exam and went to work for a Wall Street law firm (he never formally earned a degree from Columbia).

In 1910 Roosevelt left law for politics. Running as a Democrat, he narrowly won a seat in the state senate. After only two years, though, he accepted an appointment to serve as undersecretary of the Navy in the administration of Woodrow Wilson. Roosevelt spent the next several years serving his country in that capacity. Dedicated and talented, he performed particularly important work during World War I, when the nation's armed forces were mobilized to fight in Europe. Roosevelt was a reluctant administrator during this time, however. He tried on several occasions to leave his civilian post to join the U.S. military, but each time he was persuaded to remain in the administration.

Political Future Threatened by Affair and Illness

In the fall of 1918, Eleanor Roosevelt discovered that her husband was engaged in a romantic affair with Lucy Mercer, a former employee of the family. Hurt and angry, she threatened to divorce him. Franklin knew that a divorce would hurt his political career. In addition, his mother warned him to repair his marriage or risk losing the rich inheritance he was set to receive when she died. He vowed to end the affair—a promise he later broke—and Eleanor agreed to remain with him. The painful event left a permanent stain on their marriage. Afterward, though, Eleanor became more independent and outspoken, and these attributes later became hallmarks of her years as First Lady.

In 1920 Roosevelt became the Democrats' vice presidential nominee on a ticket headed by James. M. Cox, the governor of Ohio. The Republican ticket of Warren G. Harding and Calvin Coolidge won the election that fall, but Roosevelt acquitted himself well during the campaign. Many political observers pegged him as the best hope for the Democrats to reclaim the White House when the 1924 presidential election came around.

Within a matter of months, however, another dark shadow fell over Roosevelt's life. In August 1921 he was afflicted with polio, a viral disease that in its most severe forms can cause paralysis. Roosevelt lost the use of his legs because of the disease, and he was forced to use a wheelchair or heavy crutchlike braces for the rest of his life.

Many people would have retreated from public life in the face of such a crushing blow, but Roosevelt refused to surrender his dreams. Instead, he remained active in Democratic politics, and in 1928 he was elected governor of New York.

From Governor to President

Roosevelt became governor just as the Great Depression was settling over America and the world. But he approached this threat with an energy and confidence that contrasted markedly with the sluggish performance of President Herbert Hoover and other national political leaders. Declaring his belief that "the duty of the State toward the citizens is the duty of the servant to its master,"[1] Roosevelt mobilized the resources of the state to combat rising levels of hunger, poverty, and business closings. His most important move was to create a Temporary Emergency Relief Administration (TERA) in 1931. This state agency provided badly needed housing, food, clothing, and job hunting assistance to hard-hit citizens. TERA was a huge success, and Roosevelt's overall efforts to shield New York citizens from some of the worst aspects of the Depression further burnished his national reputation.

In the summer of 1932 Roosevelt became the Democratic nominee for president. A few months later, he easily defeated Hoover, whose policies during the early Depression were widely viewed as weak and uncaring. Roosevelt received 22.8 million votes—7 million more than Hoover received—and won 42 states.

When Roosevelt was sworn in as America's 32nd president on March 4, 1933, he assured the nation that "the only thing we have to fear is fear itself." From that point forward, he acted decisively to address the nation's many woes, which included widespread bank failures, massive unemployment, rising hunger, skyrocketing farm foreclosures, and mounting social unrest. In what became known as "The First Hundred Days" of his administration, Roosevelt signed numerous executive orders and persuaded Congress to pass a flurry of laws designed to bind the country's many wounds. Roosevelt believed that his legislative agenda, which he termed a "New Deal" for the American people, could reverse the nation's frightening social and economic slide.

Some of the efforts of the president and his fellow New Dealers worked better than others. But the sheer energy and vigor with which Roosevelt pursued his agenda convinced millions of Americans that the nation would be able to weather the economic storm. "The admirable trait in Roosevelt is that he has the guts to try," said Republican Senator Hiram Johnson. "He does it all with the rarest good nature.... We have exchanged for a frown in the White House a smile. Where there were hesitation and vacillation, weighing always the personal political consequences, feebleness, timidity, and duplicity, there are now courage and boldness and real action."[2]

Roosevelt's "Alphabet" Agencies

As his first term continued, Roosevelt reshaped the infrastructure of the federal government in order to revive the national economy and keep ailing families from losing all hope. He oversaw the establishment of a multitude of new agencies, including the National Recovery Administration (NRA), the Public Works Administration (PWA), the Tennessee Valley Authority (TVA), the Civilian Conservation Corps (CCC), the Federal Emergency Relief Administration (FERA), the Civil Works Administration (CWA), and the Works Progress Administration (WPA).

The missions of these agencies focused in one way or another on revitalizing American businesses and putting unemployed workers back on the job—often building schools, dams, hospitals, highways, courthouses, and other public works. "[Roosevelt] dramatized the role of the federal government," explained one scholar, "so that people would see it not as a remote and passive power but as a force that could salvage them and shape the nation's economy."[3]

Roosevelt's so-called alphabet agencies did relieve a great deal of the suffering, but they ultimately failed to stamp out the Depression. Many industries continued to struggle, unemployment rates remained high in most regions of the country, and economic fear and anxiety continued to shadow millions of families. Events such as the Dust Bowl, which destroyed millions of acres of farmland, further complicated the efforts of Roosevelt to get the nation back on its feet.

But most historians refuse to call Roosevelt's New Deal a failure. They note that most New Deal efforts did, on balance, help to reduce hunger and poverty and spur economic growth in many parts of the country. Agencies such as the WPA and CCC also took millions of men and women out of the unemployed ranks and put them to work building airports, dams, highways, and schools that became cornerstones of American economic prosperity in the second half of the twentieth century. Without this kind of federal intervention, millions of Americans would have suffered much more deeply during the Depression.

In addition, some elements of Roosevelt's New Deal had a lasting positive impact on future generations of Americans. In 1935, for example, Roosevelt signed both the National Labor Relations Act (NLRA) and the Social Security Act. The NLRA gave American workers important new legal rights to unionize and bargain collectively. The Social Security Act, meanwhile, set up a federal system that guaranteed financial assistance to elderly people, dependent children, and disabled Americans. Nearly three-quarters of a century after it was established, Social Security remained one of the nation's most important—and universally popular—federal programs.

Friend and Ally to the Common Man

Roosevelt was re-elected three times by the American people, so he served from 1933 until his death in April 1945 (the Twenty-Second Amendment to the U.S. Constitution, which limited presidents to two four-year terms, did not become law until 1951). He managed these three victories despite strong opposition from conservatives and big business executives, who distrusted Roosevelt and condemned his New Deal policies for being too harsh on business. These and other affluent critics charged that his policies unfairly penalized successful Americans and gave undeserved aid to people who simply needed to work harder to better their lives.

Roosevelt was able to triumph over this opposition because he enjoyed strong support from America's poor and working class. They knew that his New Deal programs benefited them, and they expressed their appreciation in the voting booth. "Every house I visited—mill worker or unemployed—had a picture of the President [on their walls]," recalled one New Deal official. "And the feeling of these people for the President is one of the most remarkable phenomena I have ever met. He is at once God and their intimate friend; he knows them all by name, knows their little town and mill, their little lives and problems. And though everything else fails, he is there, and will not let them down."[4]

Roosevelt's close relationship with America's working people was due in part to his ability to communicate with them in ways that made them feel comfortable and respected. His greatest tool in this regard were his fireside chats, a series of radio addresses that he made to national audiences during his years in the White House. "He was the first great American radio voice," asserted one historian. "For most Americans of this generation, their first memory of politics would be sitting by a radio and hearing *that* voice, strong, confident, totally at ease.... Most Americans in the previous 160 years had never even seen a President; now almost all of them were hearing him, *in their own homes*. It was literally and figuratively electrifying."[5]

Leading the Nation in War

When World War II erupted in 1939, Roosevelt knew that most Americans did not want to become directly involved. He thus limited the U.S. role to one of providing military and economic assistance to Great Britain and the other Allied powers fighting Japan and Nazi Germany. But after Japan attacked the U.S. base at Pearl Harbor on December 7, 1941, the tide of American public opinion changed dramatically. Roosevelt led the United States into the war, and over the next three years he oversaw America's industrial transformation into the "arsenal of democracy."

Some of Roosevelt's wartime policies have been heavily criticized, including his willingness to restrict citizens' First Amendment free speech rights and his 1942 decision to confine 110,000 Japanese Americans in internment camps for the duration of the war. But these blatant civil liberties violations received only light criticism, because most Americans were more concerned about winning the war.

As World War II continued, the huge wartime demand for military equipment and supplies restored the American economy to good health. It also made Roosevelt's New Deal programs and agencies unnecessary, so he quietly dismantled many of them. By early 1945 it was clear that the United States and its fellow Allies were going to win the war. But Roosevelt did not live to see Germany and Japan surrender later that year. He died of a massive cerebral hemorrhage on April 12 while vacationing in Georgia. His vice president, Harry S. Truman, was quickly sworn in as the nation's 33rd president. Roosevelt, meanwhile, was taken home to Hyde Park, where he was buried. His passing was mourned by millions of Americans, who credited him with providing firm and inspiring leadership during some of the nation's darkest days.

Sources:
Collier, Peter. *The Roosevelts: An American Saga*. New York: Simon and Schuster, 1994.

Davis, Kenneth S. *FDR: The New Deal Years, 1933-1937*. New York: Random House, 1986.

Goodwin, Doris Kearns. *No Ordinary Time: Franklin and Eleanor Roosevelt: The Home Front*. New York: Simon & Schuster, 1994.

Hunt, John G., ed. *The Essential Franklin D. Roosevelt*. New York: Gramercy Books, 1995.

Leuchtenberg, William E. *The FDR Years: On Roosevelt and His Legacy*. New York: Columbia University Press, 1995.

Notes:

[1] Quoted in Polenberg, Richard. *The Era of Franklin D. Roosevelt, 1933-1945: A Brief History with Documents*. Boston: Bedford/St. Martin's, 2000, p. 7.

[2] Quoted in Leuchtenberg, William E. *The FDR Years: On Roosevelt and His Legacy*. New York: Columbia University Press, 1995, p. 7.

[3] Burns, James MacGregor. *Presidential Government: The Crucible of Leadership*. Boston: Houghton Mifflin, 1966, p. 200.

[4] Quoted in Tugwell, Rexford G. "The Experimental Roosevelt," *Political Quarterly,* July-September 1950, p. 262.

[5] Halberstam, David. *The Powers That Be*. New York: Knopf, 1979, p. 15.

Henry A. Wallace (1888-1965)
Secretary of Agriculture during the Great Depression and Vice President during World War II

Henry Agard Wallace was born on October 7, 1888, on a farm in rural Adair County, Iowa. His family was the closest thing that America had to farming royalty during that era. His grandfather was the founder of *Wallace's Farmer,* a weekly agricultural newspaper that was popular in farming communities across the country. In addition, his father, Henry C. Wallace, was a nationally known voice on farming issues. He served as secretary of agriculture for Republican presidents Warren G. Harding and Calvin Coolidge in the 1920s.

Young Henry attended Iowa State College in Ames. After graduating in 1910 he joined the staff of *Wallace's Farmer.* As Wallace learned the newspaper trade, he also conducted important research on a wide range of farming issues, including the development of new breeds of high-yield corn and statistical methods for forecasting future commodity prices. In 1924 he was named managing editor of *Wallace's Farmer,* and he served in that position for the next five years.

Member of Roosevelt's Inner Circle

Wallace's life underwent major changes during the late 1920s and early 1930s. In 1929 he gave up the editorial reins at *Wallace's Farmer* to take over as publisher. Around this same time, he became much more involved in national politics. He completed a long but steady drift away from the Republican Party, which his family had always staunchly supported, and allied himself with the Democratic Party. This shift in political orientation was due primarily to Wallace's deep unhappiness with Republican farm policies, which he believed were coldhearted and ineffective.

Wallace became an outspoken critic of Republican President Herbert Hoover during the early 1930s, when the Great Depression slammed America's social and economic institutions with devastating force. His words caught the attention of Democratic power brokers, who recognized that the Wallace name still carried a lot of weight with voters in America's heartland. When Franklin D. Roosevelt defeated Hoover in the November 1932 presidential election, the president-elect asked Wallace to join his cabinet as agriculture secretary. Wallace gladly accepted the offer to follow in his father's footsteps, and in 1933 he moved to Washington, D.C., to begin his new duties.

As secretary of agriculture, Wallace was the most visible member of Roosevelt's cabinet on farm issues. His administrative duties included devising and implementing a wide range of New Deal programs designed to help farmers withstand—and ultimately recover from—the Great Depression. Some of these measures were extremely controversial, such as the Roosevelt administration's decision to boost the price of corn, wheat, and other commodities by paying farmers to cut production. This strategy did provide many farmers with desperately needed income. But it angered some Americans who argued that it was crazy to reduce food production at a time when people were going hungry.

During the next few years, Wallace became one of Roosevelt's most trusted advisors. He also emerged as one of the most dedicated and talented administrators of the New Deal. He made the Department of Agriculture into a model of efficiency for other federal agencies to follow, even though it expanded dramatically in size—from 40,000 to 140,000 employees—during his seven years at the helm. In addition, Wallace played an important role in shaping a wide range of New Deal programs, including the Agricultural Adjustment Administration, the Rural Electrification Administration, the Farm Credit Administration, the Soil Conservation Service, and federal food stamp and school lunch initiatives.

Spokesman for the New Deal

Wallace was not a gifted public speaker. But his integrity and his clear concern for the well-being of poor Americans, whether they hailed from rural farms or industrial cities, made him very popular with Roosevelt's working-class base. "Most striking of all," according to one biography, "was [Wallace's] zeal and sense of purpose. He brought to his task the solemn dedication of a crusading reformer. It was this quality that let Wallace rise above his personal reticence."[1]

In fact, by the mid-1930s Wallace ranked second only to Roosevelt himself as a champion of the New Deal. He fully believed that the federal government had both a right and a responsibility to ensure that all Americans had food, clothing, and shelter. Wallace even asserted that the New Deal's expansion of government involvement in the daily affairs of business and society reflected a Christian duty to assist one's fellow man. "We must invent, build and put to work new social machinery," he wrote in his 1934 book *New Frontiers*. "This machinery will carry out the Sermon on the Mount as well as the present social machinery carries out and intensifies the law of the jungle."[2]

In the late 1930s Wallace also became an important advisor to Roosevelt on international issues. Wallace was frightened by the rise of fascist dictatorships in Germany, Japan, and Italy, and he fiercely disagreed with "isolationist" Americans who wanted to minimize U.S. involvement with the rest of the world. Wallace believed that if fascism went unchallenged in Europe and Asia, it would someday threaten American democracy at home. When World War II broke out in early 1939, Wallace applauded Roosevelt's decision to send huge amounts of military and financial aid to the Allies.

Vice President during World War II

When Roosevelt decided to run for a third term in 1940, he selected Wallace as his running mate. The choice made sense in many respects. Wallace shared the president's genuine commitment to poor and working-class Americans, he deeply believed in the principles that drove the New Deal, and he had the same outlook as Roosevelt on most international issues. Most important of all, Roosevelt was convinced that if he was unable to complete his term because of death or illness, the nation would be in good hands with Wallace.

The selection of Wallace met with some opposition from some Democratic Party leaders, however. They felt that "he was too idealistic to be a good politician, that he did not have a wide following, and that he was in essence too much like Roosevelt to balance the ticket," according to one scholar.[3] But when Roosevelt threatened to drop out of the race entirely if they did not approve his selection of Wallace, party leaders immediately dropped their complaints. The Roosevelt-Wallace ticket won the 1940 election, carrying 55 percent of the popular vote and 38 states.

During the next four years, Wallace was an influential and active force in shaping and carrying out administration policies. Unlike many previous vice presidents, he was given important responsibilities. After the United States entered World War II in December 1941, for example, he headed the powerful Board of Economic Warfare.

Wallace maintained a close friendship with the president throughout the early 1940s. During these years, though, he expressed growing concerns that the war was distracting Roosevelt from important social reforms that had yet to be accomplished at home. Meanwhile, Wallace's progressive beliefs and his calls for international cooperation to achieve a "Century of the Common Man" revived fears among some Democrats that he was becoming too controversial. As the 1944 elections approached, they demanded that Roosevelt replace Wallace with a less liberal vice presidential candidate. Roosevelt reluctantly agreed in the interests of party unity. He parted ways with Wallace and named Harry S. Truman as his running mate. But as soon as Roosevelt won his fourth term, he appointed Wallace as his new secretary of commerce.

When Roosevelt died in April 1945, Wallace stayed on at the Commerce Department to help Truman make the transition to the presidency. Wallace left one year later, though, and over the next several years he became a persistent critic of the Truman administration's Cold War policies. In 1948 he ran for president as the nominee of the Progressive Party, but he received only 2.4 percent of the popular vote. Wallace then retired from political life. He spent his remaining years gardening and exploring various scientific farming techniques at his large farm in New York state. He died on November 18, 1965, in Danbury, Connecticut.

Sources:

Culver, John C., and John Hyde. *American Dreamer: A Life of Henry A. Wallace.* New York: W.W. Norton, 2001.

Markowitz, Norman D. *The Rise and Fall of the People's Century: Henry A. Wallace and American Liberalism, 1941-1948.* New York: Free Press, 1973.

Wallace, Henry A. *New Frontiers.* New York: Reynal and Hitchcock, 1934.

Notes:

1 Culver, John C., and John Hyde. *American Dreamer: A Life of Henry A. Wallace.* New York: W.W. Norton, 2001, p. 128.

2 Wallace, Henry A. *New Frontiers.* New York: Reynal and Hitchcock, 1934, p. 11.

3 Woolner, David B. Biography of Henry A. Wallace. *View from Hyde Park,* Summer 2001.

PRIMARY SOURCES

Remembering a Depression Childhood

The celebrated American poet Philip Levine was born in 1928, one year before the Great Depression struck. A short time later his father died, leaving Levine's mother to support him and his older brother from the modest money she earned as a stenographer. In the following excerpt from his critically acclaimed memoir, The Bread of Time, *Levine recalls his memories of growing up in Detroit, Michigan, during the height of the Depression.*

Entering the second grade that year, I began to notice for the first time how differently we students dressed, and at the same time how many of us wore the same clothes. There were four boys in my class aside from me who wore sweaters which bore the figure of a stag knitted in white against a maroon background. It too had been on sale at Hudson's, the maroon a dollar cheaper than the navy blue. There was one boy who wore far more elegant sweaters in subtle hues of brown and fawn; even his checked socks were in matching colors. He was always neatly combed, his nails were never bitten down, and they gleamed as though they had been polished. I noticed too that my teacher seemed to defer to him, to call on him only when he raised is hand and clearly knew the answers to her questions, whereas she was continually trying to make fools out of the rest of us. This boy, Milton Journey, was always driven to school in a long white La Salle convertible, which I learned belonged to his older brother, who attended a nearby junior high school. On winter days, after school, Milton would wait in his long blue overcoat inside the main doors until his mother stopped and honked from her sedan. Milton would toss back his straight blond hair, shrug, and go out into the weather to accept his privileges.

Another boy, Fred Batten, disgusted me. When he spoke to me he had a habit of sticking his face as close as he could to mine, as though he were trying to swipe my breath; perhaps he truly meant to, for his own breath smelled awful. Unfortunately he had some sort of affection for me and constantly pursued me. One day I noticed that the skin behind his ears and around his neck bore dark smudges. I realized Fred Batten didn't wash; his hands too were always filthy. With a shock I realized that he wore no socks, and often that winter the skin of his ankles was raw and swollen. One day he caught me staring at his bare ankles, and he turned away from me in silence. I began to notice several other boys and girls who bore these same "wounds" at wrist and ankles, and I did my best not to stare at them.

Winters in Michigan were fierce, but I never left for school without a warm jacket, socks, a cap that covered my ears, usually by means of some sort of hideous flap that fastened below the chin, gloves, and a scarf. Not once did I go off without a sacked lunch, nor were lice ever found in my hair, though weekly I had to bow for the health officer's inspection. Many of my classmates were not so fortunate and were taken off for their "treatment" and returned, heads bent and reeking of kerosene.

Lunchtimes grew particularly difficult, for many students had nothing to eat except for the free carton of milk that was provided by the school. By the age of ten I'd decided that it was easier to walk the mile back to our apartment and eat my lunch in privacy than to bear the envious glances of many of my schoolmates. In autumn especially the tree-lined streets were lovely, and since my mother was unable to buy glasses for me until I was fourteen, in those early years I was walking through a city invented by an impressionist painter.

Often I'd make the walk home with a classmates, Martin Peters, who though shorter than I was actually two years older and lived with his family in a "halfer," a second-story apartment that was divided into separate units both of which shared the kitchen and bathroom. Suddenly, during a particularly cold week in January, Martin stopped coming to school. I didn't see him for three weeks. The word was he was suffering from pneumonia, but when he returned to class he shared his secret. His mother had been keeping him home because he had no heavy jacket or coat. His father was out of work, the gas bill had not been paid, so the heat had been shut off. Martin had spent most days in bed, under the covers, listening to the radio. During those weeks he'd become an extraordinary source of the comings and goings of his favorite soap-opera characters, and now the need to return to class was depriving him of more of their adventures.

Something was very wrong with the world, and I was powerless to do anything about it. When my father died in his middle thirties I was assured that it was due to the rules of God: the good died young so that they could be close to Him. That did me and my family absolutely no good, for we were doomed to spend the rest of our lives deprived of this lovable man. Poor men came to our doors daily, and we had to turn them away for lack of anything to give them. To and from school I would walk past blocks of stately mansions. I experimented. In the back seat of my grandfather's Hudson, I would imagine myself equipped with a repeating rifle and opening fire on every Cadillac, La Salle, Lincoln, or Chrysler we happened across. This was my battle against the forces of injustice and greed. My bullets equalized nothing, but they made me feel better....

When I was seven my mother hired a hill woman named Florence Hickok to clean, cook, and look after us, especially during the summer, when we were out of school and my mother worked all though the season as a stenographer. Florence was one of those uncompromising Americans who believe in militancy, a fair wage, and the never-ending battle against the excesses of capitalism that all decent working people were obliged by God and common sense to carry on until their last breath. Tall, gaunt, weather-beaten, with a cigarette burning in the corner of her mouth, at the breakfast table she'd read through the morning *Free Press* muttering, "The bastards are selling us down the river." She hadn't the least doubt that the European "democracies" and America as well were run by and for the rich. By "us" she meant, of course, all those who had to work for a living, whose labor created the wealth that ironically imprisoned them. From the Black Hills of the Dakotas, Florence claimed to be of the same blood as Wild Bill [Hickok], who she assured us was also a red. (In those days independent working Americans were proud of being red, which did not mean membership in the Communist Party [CP]: it merely meant struggling with the common people against the exploiters. No matter what you've been told to the contrary, we reds knew the difference between the totalitarian, brainwashed CP members, the professional Communists, and ourselves, the reds who wanted not to be encumbered with another hierarchy of bosses.)

Source: Levine, Philip. *The Bread of Time: Toward an Autobiography.* New York: Alfred A. Knopf, 1994.

Herbert Hoover Predicts a Quick Recovery

Throughout most of his presidency, Herbert Hoover rejected calls to initiate large-scale government programs to fight the Depression. He believed that the nation's economic woes would correct themselves over time, and he argued that federal unemployment relief programs and other types of government intervention would ultimately hurt the country. Instead, Hoover urged religious and charitable organizations to take care of the needs of the nation's swelling ranks of homeless and unemployed, and he called on Americans to exercise "mutual self-help." Hoover touched on all of these themes in this October 18, 1931, radio address to the nation.

My fellow citizens:

This broadcast tonight marks the beginning of the mobilization of the whole Nation for a great undertaking to provide security for those of our citizens and their families who, through no fault of their own, face unemployment and privation during the coming winter. Its success depends upon the sympathetic and generous action of every man and woman in our country. No one with a spark of human sympathy can contemplate unmoved the possibilities of suffering that can crush many of our unfortunate fellow Americans if we shall fail them.

The depression has been deepened by events from abroad which are beyond the control either of our citizens or our Government. Although it is but a passing incident in our national life, we must meet the consequences in unemployment which arise from it with that completeness of effort and that courage and spirit for which citizenship in this Nation always has and always must stand.

As an important part of our plans for national unity of action in this emergency I have created a great national organization under the leadership of Mr. Walter Gifford to cooperate with the Governors, the State and the local agencies, and with the many national organizations of business, of labor, and of welfare, with the churches and our fraternal and patriotic societies so that the countless streams of human helpfulness which have been the mainstay of our country in all emergencies may be directed wisely and effectively.

Over a thousand towns and cities have well-organized and experienced unemployment relief committees, community chests, or other agencies for the efficient administration of this relief. With this occasion begins the nationwide movement to aid each of these volunteer organizations in securing the funds to meet their task over the forthcoming winter.

158

This organized effort is our opportunity to express our sympathy, to lighten the burdens of the heavy laden, and to cast sunshine into the habitation of despair.

The amounts sought by the committee in your town or city are in part to provide work, for it is through work that we wish to give help in keeping with the dignity of American manhood and womanhood. But much of their funds are necessary to provide direct relief to those families where circumstances and ill fortune can only be met by direct assistance. Included in many community appeals are the sums necessary to the vital measures of health and character building, the maintenance of which were never more necessary than in these times.

The Federal Government is taking its part in aid to unemployment through the advancement and enlargement of public works in all parts of the Nation. Through these works, it is today providing a livelihood for nearly 700,000 families. All immigration has been stopped in order that our burdens should not be increased by unemployed immigrants from abroad. Measures have been adopted which will assure normal credits and thus stimulate employment in industry, in commerce, and in agriculture. The employers in national industries have spread work amongst their employees so that the maximum number may participate in the wages which are available. Our States, our counties, our municipalities, through the expansion of their public works and through tax-supported relief activities, are doing their full part. Yet, beyond all this, there is a margin of relief which must be provided by voluntary action. Through these agencies Americans must meet the demands of national conscience that there be no hunger or cold amongst our people.

Similar organization and generous support were provided during the past winter in localities where it was necessary. Under the leadership of Colonel Woods, we succeeded in the task of that time. We demonstrated that it could be done. But in many localities our need will be greater this winter than a year ago. While many are affected by the depression, the number who are threatened with privation is a minor percentage of our whole people.

This task is not beyond the ability of these thousands of community organizations to solve. Each local organization from its experience last winter and summer has formulated careful plans and made estimates completely to meet the need of that community. I am confident that the generosity of each community will fully support these estimates. The sum of these community efforts will meet the needs of the Nation as a whole.

To solve this problem in this way accords with the fundamental sense of responsibility, neighbor to neighbor, community to community, upon which our Nation is founded.

The possible misery of helpless people gives me more concern than any other trouble that this depression has brought upon us. It is with these convictions in mind that I have the responsibility of opening this nationwide appeal to citizens in each community that they provide the funds with which, community by community, this task shall be met.

The maintenance of a spirit of mutual self-help through voluntary giving, through the responsibility of local government, is of infinite importance to the future of America. Everyone who aids to the full extent of his ability is giving support to the very foundations of our democracy. Everyone who from a sympathetic heart gives to these services is giving hope and courage to some deserving family. Everyone who aids in this service will have lighted a beacon of help on the stormy coast of human adversity.

The success and the character of nations are to be judged by the ideals and the spirit of its people. Time and again the American people have demonstrated a spiritual quality, a capacity for unity of action, of generosity, a certainty of results in time of emergency that have made them great in the annals of the history of all nations. This is the time and this is the occasion when we must arouse that idealism, that spirit, that determination, that unity of action, from which there can be no failure in this primary obligation of every man to his neighbor and of a nation to its citizens, that none who deserve shall suffer.

I would that I possessed the art of words to fix the real issue with which the troubled world is faced in the mind and heart of every American man and woman. Our country and the world are today involved in more than a financial crisis. We are faced with the primary question of human relations, which reaches to the very depths of organized society and to the very depths of human conscience. This civilization and this great complex, which we call American life, is builded and can alone survive upon the translation into individual action of that fundamental philosophy announced by the Savior 19 centuries ago. Part of our national suffering today is from failure to observe these primary yet inexorable laws of human relationship. Modern society cannot survive with the defense of Cain, "Am I my brother's keeper ?"

No governmental action, no economic doctrine, no economic plan or project can replace that God-imposed responsibility of the individual man and woman to their neighbors. That is a vital part of the very soul of a people. If we shall gain in this spirit from this painful time, we shall have created a greater and more glorious America. The trial of it is here now. It is a trial of the heart and the conscience, of individual men and women.

In a little over a month we shall celebrate our time-honored festival of Thanksgiving. I appeal to the American people to make November 26 next the outstanding Thanksgiving Day in the history of the United States; that we may say on that day that America has again demonstrated her ideals; that we have each of us contributed our full part; that we in each of our communities have given full assurance against hunger and cold amongst our people; that upon this Thanksgiving Day we have removed the fear of the forthcoming winter from the hearts of all who are suffering and in distress—that we are our brother's keeper.

I am on my way to participate in the commemoration of the victory of Yorktown. It is a name which brings a glow of pride to every American. It recalls the final victory of our people after years of sacrifice and privation. This Nation passed through Valley Forge and came to Yorktown.

Source: John T. Woolley and Gerhard Peters, The American Presidency Project [online]. Santa Barbara, CA: University of California (hosted), Gerhard Peters (database). Available online at http://www.presidency.ucsb.edu/ws/?pid=22855.

Franklin D. Roosevelt's First Inaugural Address

On March 4th, 1933, Franklin D. Roosevelt was sworn in as the thirty-second president of the United States. In his inauguration speech to the American people, he acknowledged that the nation was in the grip of serious economic and social problems. But he expressed great optimism about America's capacity to overcome those difficulties, and he promised to take decisive steps to address what he called a "national emergency." Following is the text of Roosevelt's historic speech:

I am certain that my fellow Americans expect that on my induction into the Presidency I will address them with a candor and a decision which the present situation of our Nation impels. This is preeminently the time to speak the truth, the whole truth, frankly and boldly. Nor need we shrink from honestly facing conditions in our country today. This great Nation will endure as it has endured, will revive and will prosper. So, first of all, let me assert my firm belief that the only thing we have to fear is fear itself—nameless, unreasoning, unjustified terror which paralyzes needed efforts to convert retreat into advance. In every dark hour of our national life a leadership of frankness and vigor has met with that understanding and support of the people themselves which is essential to victory. I am convinced that you will again give that support to leadership in these critical days.

In such a spirit on my part and on yours we face our common difficulties. They concern, thank God, only material things. Values have shrunken to fantastic levels; taxes have risen; our ability to pay has fallen; government of all kinds is faced by serious curtailment of income; the means of exchange are frozen in the currents of trade; the withered leaves of industrial enterprise lie on every side; farmers find no markets for their produce; the savings of many years in thousands of families are gone.

More important, a host of unemployed citizens face the grim problem of existence, and an equally great number toil with little return. Only a foolish optimist can deny the dark realities of the moment.

Yet our distress comes from no failure of substance. We are stricken by no plague of locusts. Compared with the perils which our forefathers conquered because they believed and were not afraid, we have still much to be thankful for. Nature still offers her bounty and human efforts have multiplied it. Plenty is at our doorstep, but a generous use of it languishes in the very sight of the supply. Primarily this is because rulers of the exchange of mankind's goods have failed through their own stubbornness and their own incompetence, have admitted their failure, and have abdicated. Practices of the unscrupulous money changers stand indicted in the court of public opinion, rejected by the hearts and minds of men.

True they have tried, but their efforts have been cast in the pattern of an outworn tradition. Faced by failure of credit they have proposed only the lending of more money. Stripped of the lure of profit by which to induce our people to follow their false leadership, they have resorted to exhortations, pleading tearfully for restored confidence. They know only the rules of a generation of self-seekers. They have no vision, and when there is no vision the people perish.

The money changers have fled from their high seats in the temple of our civilization. We may now restore that temple to the ancient truths. The measure of the restoration lies in the extent to which we apply social values more noble than mere monetary profit.

Happiness lies not in the mere possession of money; it lies in the joy of achievement, in the thrill of creative effort. The joy and moral stimulation of work no longer must be forgotten in the mad chase of evanescent profits. These dark days will be worth all they cost us if they teach us that our true destiny is not to be ministered unto but to minister to ourselves and to our fellow men.

Recognition of the falsity of material wealth as the standard of success goes hand in hand with the abandonment of the false belief that public office and high political position are to be valued only by the standards of pride of place and personal profit; and there must be an end to a conduct in banking and in business which too often has given to a sacred trust the likeness of callous and selfish wrongdoing. Small wonder that confidence languishes, for it thrives only on honesty, on honor, on the sacredness of obligations, on faithful protection, on unselfish performance; without them it cannot live. Restoration calls, however, not for changes in ethics alone. This Nation asks for action, and action now.

Our greatest primary task is to put people to work. This is no unsolvable problem if we face it wisely and courageously. It can be accomplished in part by direct recruiting by the Government itself, treating the task as we would treat the emergency of a war, but at the same time, through this employment, accomplishing greatly needed projects to stimulate and reorganize the use of our natural resources.

Hand in hand with this we must frankly recognize the overbalance of population in our industrial centers and, by engaging on a national scale in a redistribution, endeavor to provide a better use of the land for those best fitted for the land. The task can be helped by definite efforts to raise the values of agricultural products and with this the power to purchase the output of our cities. It can be helped by preventing realistically the tragedy of the growing loss through foreclosure of our small homes and our farms. It can be helped by insistence that the Federal, State, and local governments act forthwith on the demand that their cost be drastically reduced. It can be helped by the unifying of relief activities which today are often scattered, uneconomical, and unequal. It can be helped by national planning for and supervision of all forms of transportation and of communications and other utilities which have a definitely public character. There are many ways in which it can be helped, but it can never be helped merely by talking about it. We must act and act quickly.

Finally, in our progress toward a resumption of work we require two safeguards against a return of the evils of the old order: there must be a strict supervision of all banking and credits and investments, so that there will be an end to speculation with other people's money; and there must be provision for an adequate but sound currency.

These are the lines of attack. I shall presently urge upon a new Congress, in special session, detailed measures for their fulfillment, and I shall seek the immediate assistance of the several States.

Through this program of action we address ourselves to putting our own national house in order and making income balance outgo. Our international trade relations, though vastly important, are in point of time and necessity secondary to the establishment of a sound national economy. I favor as a practical policy the putting of first things first. I shall spare no effort to restore world trade by international economic readjustment, but the emergency at home cannot wait on that accomplishment.

The basic thought that guides these specific means of national recovery is not narrowly nationalistic. It is the insistence, as a first considerations, upon the interdependence of the various elements in and parts of the United States—a recognition of the old and permanently important manifestation of the American spirit of the pioneer. It is the way to recovery. It is the immediate way. It is the strongest assurance that the recovery will endure.

In the field of world policy I would dedicate this Nation to the policy of the good neighbor—the neighbor who resolutely respects himself and, because he does so, respects the rights of others—the neighbor who respects his obligations and respects the sanctity of his agreements in and with a world of neighbors.

If I read the temper of our people correctly, we now realize as we have never realized before our interdependence on each other; that we cannot merely take but we must give as well; that if we are to go forward, we must move as a trained and loyal army willing to sacrifice for the good of a common discipline, because without such discipline no progress is made, no leadership becomes effective. We are, I know, ready and willing to submit our lives and property to such discipline, because it makes possible a leadership which aims at a larger good. This I propose to offer, pledging that the larger purposes will bind upon us all as a sacred obligation with a unity of duty hitherto evoked only in time of armed strife.

With this pledge taken, I assume unhesitatingly the leadership of this great army of our people dedicated to a disciplined attack upon our common problems.

Action in this image and to this end is feasible under the form of government which we have inherited from our ancestors. Our Constitution is so simple and practical that it is possible always to meet extraordinary needs by changes in emphasis and arrangement without loss of essential form. That is why our constitutional system has proved itself the most superbly enduring political mechanism the modern world has produced. It has met every stress of vast expansion of territory, of foreign wars, of bitter internal strife, of world relations.

It is to be hoped that the normal balance of Executive and legislative authority may be wholly adequate to meet the unprecedented task before us. But it may be that an unprecedented demand and need for undelayed action may call for temporary departure from that normal balance of public procedure.

I am prepared under my constitutional duty to recommend the measures that a stricken Nation in the midst of a stricken world may require. These measures, or such other measures as the Congress may build out of its experience and wisdom, I shall seek, within my constitutional authority, to bring to speedy adoption.

But in the event that the Congress shall fail to take one of these two courses, and in the event that the national emergency is still critical, I shall not evade the clear course of duty that will then confront me. I shall ask the

Congress for the one remaining instrument to meet the crisis-broad Executive power to wage a war against the emergency, as great as the power that would be given to me if we were in fact invaded by a foreign foe.

For the trust reposed in me I will return the courage and the devotion that befit the time. I can do no less.

We face the arduous days that lie before us in the warm courage of national unity; with the clear consciousness of seeking old and precious moral values; with the clean satisfaction that comes from the stern performance of duty by old and young alike. We aim at the assurance of a rounded and permanent national life.

We do not distrust the future of essential democracy. The people of the United States have not failed. In their need they have registered a mandate that they want direct, vigorous action. They have asked for discipline and direction under leadership. They have made me the present instrument of their wishes. In the spirit of the gift I take it.

In this dedication of a Nation we humbly ask the blessing of God. May He protect each and every one of us. May He guide me in the days to come.

Source: John T. Woolley and Gerhard Peters, The American Presidency Project [online]. Santa Barbara, CA: University of California (hosted), Gerhard Peters (database). Available online at http://www.presidency.ucsb.edu/ws/?pid=14473.

Praise for the Civilian Conservation Corps

One of the first major New Deal programs was the Civilian Conservation Corps (CCC), a public works employment initiative that proved enormously popular. The program, created by an executive order signed by President Franklin D. Roosevelt on April 5, 1933, put more than three million young men to work on conservation and land development projects across the country. The following testimonial to the program's excellence was given by Keith Hufford, who worked for the CCC in Utah from 1933 through 1937.

In May, 1933, I was one of the many jobless disillusioned young men who trooped wearily and despondently into a CCC reconditioning camp, not knowing, and not particularly caring, about the future.

We, at least an overwhelming majority of us, were of a generation founded on nothing more than national economic instability, want, and hunger; with the inevitable result: Continuance of our education was impossible as well as a development of our natural talents, granting we possessed any, inasmuch as it became our duty to search for jobs—and none were available.

You must suffer the experience of tramping hot, smelly pavements day to day, going from one employment bureau to another, with the perpetual answer dinning in your ears until it becomes a satanic chorus of no!—No!—NO!!, let the hunger gnaw at your vitals until the head spins like a top and all the world becomes nothing but a whirling kaleidoscope of faces, places, streets, buildings, the sun simply a huge black disk, and some "Good Samaritan" has you thrown into the local jail for drunkenness and vagrancy. God forbid, but I repeat you must go through the actual experience before you can really understand the hopeless state of mind most of the prospective members of the CCC were in when we put on our "G.I." clothing and tramped half-heartedly into the forests and fields to plant and cut trees, build dams, lime kilns, fire breaks and trails, control insect pests, tree diseases, and risk our lives on a current of wind while protecting the forests from the most efficient of destructive forces—Fire.

But our don't-care-what-happens attitude didn't last long. A great deal of credit must be given to the boys for their ability to adjust themselves to an entirely new environment, and for the enthusiasm and zest with which they attacked a new project, anxious to get it completed and note the results, and in the meantime, secure in their knowledge the folks "back home" had a small, but helpful income.

The educational system was not in effect during what I choose to call the "infancy" of the CCC. We worked the proper number of hours and after that it was up to us to entertain ourselves in any manner deemed practicable and safe by the Commanding Officer. Before long, we were having inter-camp musical entertainments, boxing bouts, impromptu spelling bees, and quite often, interesting plays and sketches. I recall one such meeting in a camp at the foot of Mt. Lassen, Cal. [California], where we were swamped with 490 visitors in one single night.

As our organization overcame it's "growing pains," and more efficient methods were adopted for the benefit of the camps and personnel, a uniform program of education was put into effect. Young men who had of a necessity terminated their educational pursuits were in a position to take them up again, and illiterates were encouraged to learn the three "R's." Recognized correspondence schools cooperated with us by making special rates, local high schools and civic bodies offered their support, job training was given by the technical service, and even those of us who had a knowledge of some particular subject were enlisted to teach others who were interested, all we knew. It was loads of fun for everybody. A very close friend of mine, who, by saving every penny he could scrape together for four years, is now in his third year at Ohio State University, and well on his way to success.

As for me, I made my own bunk in various camps over the United States for five years. I was fortunate in obtaining a good job but finally came home. And now, I often become homesick for the noise and clamor of the mess hall where 150 ravenous boys troop in three times a day, the twang of guitars as a soft-voiced enrollee sings a plaintive mountain melody on the steps of the barrack in the soft, summer twilight, the smell of clean steaming bodies and the stinging crack of a turkish towel in the bathhouse after the day's work is done. All of these things, and many more, I long for, but I must make way for some other young fellow who needs a bracer-upper for his moral and physical self and—his soul.

I still have not attained my goal but I am making my own way and that is sufficient for the present. What is probably more important is the fact that I am not the undernourished, furtive-eyed, scared kid that went into Fort Knox over five years ago. Instead, my eyes are clear and my mind is receptive to whatever the future has in store. In short, the CCC has equipped me with the weapons necessary to cope with the innumerable problems that are bound to obstruct my path through life and that must be surmounted before success can be attained.

Keith Hufford
Former CCC Enrollee
from Harrison County

Source: "Keith Hufford, Testimonial," National Archives and Records Administration, *Success Stories,* CCC in Utah, c. 1937. Available online at New Deal Network, Franklin and Eleanor Roosevelt Institute, http://newdeal.feri.org/texts/295.htm.

An Excerpt from John Steinbeck's *The Grapes of Wrath*

In 1939 American novelist John Steinbeck published The Grapes of Wrath, *a story based on the author's first-hand impressions of the Dust Bowl.* The Grapes of Wrath *tells the story of a desperate but proud farming family's flight from Oklahoma to California during the height of the Dust Bowl years. The novel is widely regarded as a classic of American literature and Steinbeck's finest work. It remains one of the most vivid and powerful documents of the Great Depression. Following are two excerpts from the book:*

Chapter 5

The owners of the land came onto the land, or more often a spokesman for the owners came. They came in closed cars, and they felt the dry earth with their fingers, and sometimes they drove big earth augers into the ground for soil tests. The tenants, from their sun-beaten dooryards, watched uneasily when the closed cars drove along the fields. And at last the owner men drove into the dooryards and sat in their cars to talk out of the windows. The tenant men stood beside the cars for a while, and then squatted on their hams and found sticks with which to mark the dust.

In the open doors the women stood looking out, and behind them the children—corn-headed children, with wide eyes, one bare foot on top of the other bare foot, and the toes working. The women and the children watched their men talking to the owner men. They were silent.

Some of the owner men were kind because they hated what they had to do, and some of them were angry because they hated to be cruel, and some of them were cold because they had long ago found that one could not be an owner unless one were cold. And all of them were caught in something larger than themselves. Some of them hated the mathematics that drove them, and some were afraid, and some worshiped the mathematics because it provided a refuge from thought and from feeling. If a bank or a finance company owned the land, the owner man said, The Bank—or the Company—needs—wants—insists—must have—as though the Bank or the Company were a monster, with thought and feeling, which had ensnared them. These last would take no responsibility for the banks or the companies because they were men and

---

slaves, while the banks were machines and masters all at the same time. Some of the owner men were a little proud to be slaves to such cold and powerful masters. The owner men sat in the cars and explained. You know the land is poor. You've scrabbled at it long enough, God knows.

The squatting tenant men nodded and wondered and drew figures in the dust, and yes, they knew, God knows. If the dust only wouldn't fly. If the top would only stay on the soil, it might not be so bad.

The owner men went on leading to their point: You know the land's getting poorer. You know what cotton does to the land; robs it, sucks all the blood out of it.

The squatters nodded—they knew, God knew. If they could only rotate the crops they might pump blood back into the land.

Well, it's too late. And the owner men explained the workings and the thinkings of the monster that was stronger than they were. A man can hold land if he can just eat and pay taxes; he can do that.

Yes, he can do that until his crops fail one day and he has to borrow money from the bank.

But—you see, a bank or a company can't do that, because those creatures don't breathe air, don't eat side-meat. They breathe profits; they eat the interest on money. If they don't get it, they die the way you die without air, without side-meat. It is a sad thing, but it is so. It is just so.

The squatting men raised their eyes to understand. Can't we just hang on? Maybe the next year will be a good year. God knows how much cotton next year. And with all the wars—God knows what price cotton will bring. Don't they make explosives out of cotton? And uniforms? Get enough wars and cotton'll hit the ceiling. Next year, maybe. They looked up questioningly.

We can't depend on it. The bank—the monster has to have profits all the time. It can't wait. It'll die. No, taxes go on. When the monster stops growing, it dies. It can't stay one size.

Soft fingers began to tap the sill of the car window, and hard fingers tightened on the restless drawing sticks. In the doorways of the sun-beaten tenant houses, women sighed and then shifted feet so that the one that had been down was now on top, and the toes working. Dogs came sniffing near the owner cars and wetted on all four tires one after another. And chickens lay in the sunny dust and fluffed their feathers to get the cleansing dust down

171

to the skin. In the little sties the pigs grunted inquiringly over the muddy remnants of the slops.

The squatting men looked down again. What do you want us to do? We can't take less share of the crop—we're half starved now. The kids are hungry all the time. We got no clothes, torn an' ragged. If all the neighbors weren't the same, we'd be ashamed to go to meeting.

And at last the owner men came to the point. The tenant system won't work any more. One man on a tractor can take the place of twelve or fourteen families. Pay him a wage and take all the crop. We have to do it. We don't like to do it. But the monster's sick. Something's happened to the monster.

But you'll kill the land with cotton.

We know. We've got to take cotton quick before the land dies. Then we'll sell the land. Lots of families in the East would like to own a piece of land.

The tenant men looked up alarmed. But what'll happen to us? How'll we eat?

You'll have to get off the land. The plows'll go through the dooryard.

And now the squatting men stood up angrily. Grampa took up the land, and he had to kill the Indians and drive them away. And Pa was born here, and he killed weeds and snakes. Then a bad year came and he had to borrow a little money. An' we was born here. There in the door—our children born here. And Pa had to borrow money. The bank owned the land then, but we stayed and we got a little bit of what we raised.

We know that—all that. It's not us, it's the bank. A bank isn't like a man. Or an owner with fifty thousand acres, he isn't like a man either. That's the monster.

Sure, cried the tenant men, but it's our land. We measured it and broke it up. We were born on it, and we got killed on it, died on it. Even if it's no good, it's still ours. That's what makes it ours—being born on it, working it, dying on it. That makes ownership, not a paper with numbers on it.

We're sorry. It's not us. It's the monster. The bank isn't like a man.

Yes, but the bank is only made of men.

No, you're wrong there—quite wrong there. The bank is something else than men. It happens that every man in a bank hates what the bank does, and yet the bank does it. The bank is something more than men, I tell you. It's the monster. Men made it, but they can't control it.

The tenants cried, Grampa killed Indians, Pa killed snakes for the land. Maybe we can kill banks—they're worse than Indians and snakes. Maybe we got to fight to keep our land, like Pa and Grampa did.

And now the owner men grew angry. You'll have to go.

But it's ours, the tenant men cried. We—

No. The bank, the monster owns it. You'll have to go.

We'll get our guns, like Grampa when the Indians came. What then?

Well—first the sheriff, and then the troops. You'll be stealing if you try to stay, you'll be murderers if you kill to stay. The monster isn't men, but it can make men do what it wants.

But if we go, where'll we go? How'll we go? We got no money.

We're sorry, said the owner men. The bank, the fifty-thousand-acre owner can't be responsible. You're on land that isn't yours. Once over the line maybe you can pick cotton in the fall. Maybe you can go on relief. Why don't you go on west to California? There's work there, and it never gets cold. Why, you can reach out anywhere and pick an orange. Why, there's always some kind of crop to work in. Why don't you go there? And the owner men started their cars and rolled away....

Chapter 21

The moving questing people were migrants now. Those families who had lived on a little piece of land, who had lived and died on forty acres, had eaten or starved on the produce of forty acres, had now the whole West to rove in. And they scampered about, looking for work; and the highways were streams of people, and the ditch banks were lines of people. Behind them more were coming. The great highways streamed with moving people. There in the Middle- and Southwest had lived a simple agrarian folk who had not changed with industry, who had not farmed with machines or known the power and danger of machines in private hands. They had not grown up in the paradoxes of industry. Their senses were still sharp to the ridiculousness of the industrial life.

And then suddenly the machines pushed them out and they swarmed on the highways. The movement changed them; the highways, the camps along the road, the fear of hunger and the hunger itself, changed them. The children without dinner changed them, the endless moving changed them. They were migrants. And the hostility changed them, welded them, united them—hostility that made the little towns group and arm as though to repel an invader, squads with pick handles, clerks and storekeepers with shotguns, guarding the world against their own people.

In the West there was panic when the migrants multiplied on the highways. Men of property were terrified for their property. Men who had never been hungry saw the eyes of the hungry. Men who had never wanted anything very much saw the flare of want in the eyes of the migrants. And the men of the towns and of the soft suburban country gathered to defend themselves; and they reassured themselves that they were good and the invaders bad, as a man must do before he fights. They said, These goddamned Okies are dirty and ignorant. They're degenerate, sexual maniacs. Those goddamned Okies are thieves. They'll steal anything. They've got no sense of property rights.

And the latter was true, for how can a man without property know the ache of ownership? And the defending people said, They bring disease, they're filthy. We can't have them in the schools. They're strangers. How'd you like to have your sister go out with one of 'em?

The local people whipped themselves into a mold of cruelty. Then they formed units, squads, and armed them—armed them with clubs, with gas, with guns. We own the country. We can't let these Okies get out of hand. And the men who were armed did not own the land, but they thought they did. And the clerks who drilled at night owned nothing, and the little storekeepers possessed only a drawerful of debts. But even a debt is something, even a job is something. The clerk thought, I get fifteen dollars a week. S'pose a goddamn Okie would work for twelve? And the little storekeeper thought, How could I compete with a debtless man?

And the migrants streamed in on the highways and their hunger was in their eyes, and their need was in their eyes. They had no argument, no system, nothing but their numbers and their needs. When there was work for a man, ten men fought for it—fought with a low wage. If that fella'll work for thirty cents, I'll work for twenty-five.

If he'll take twenty-five, I'll do it for twenty.

No me, I'm hungry. I'll work for fifteen. I'll work for food. The kids. You ought to see them. Little boils, like, comin' out, an' they can't run aroun'. Give 'em some windfall fruit, an' they bloated up. Me, I'll work for a little piece of meat.

174

And this was good, for wages went down and prices stayed up. The great owners were glad and they sent out more handbills to bring more people in. And wages went down and prices stayed up. And pretty soon now we'll have serfs again.

And now the great owners and the companies invented a new method. A great owner bought a cannery. And when the peaches and the pears were ripe he cut the price of fruit below the cost of raising it. And as cannery owner he paid himself a low price for the fruit and kept the price of canned goods up and took his profit. And the little farmers who owned no canneries lost their farms, and they were taken by the great owners, the banks, and the companies who also owned the canneries. As time went on, there were fewer farms. The little farmers moved into town for a while and exhausted their credit, exhausted their friends, their relatives. And then they too went on the highways. And the roads were crowded with men ravenous for work, murderous for work.

And the companies, the banks worked at their own doom and they did not know it. The fields were fruitful, and starving men moved on the roads. The granaries were full and the children of the poor grew up rachitic [with diseases of the spine], and the postules of pellagra [a chronic disease caused by dietary deficiencies] swelled on their sides. The great companies did not know that the line between hunger and anger is a thin line. And money that might have gone to wages went for gas, for guns, for agents and spies, for blacklists, for drilling. On the highways the people moved like ants and searched for work, for food. And the anger began to ferment.

Source: Steinbeck, John. *The Grapes of Wrath.* New York: Viking Press, 1939.

Woody Guthrie Describes the Dust Bowl

American singer and songwriter Woody Guthrie ranks as one of the nation's music legends. Born in Okemah, Oklahoma in 1912, he grew up to write "This Land is Your Land" and many other famous songs. A life-long wanderer and political rebel until his death in a New York state hospital in 1967, Guthrie used his lyrics and guitar to champion the cause of the common man and highlight perceived political injustices in America. He was also a firsthand witness to the horrors of the Dust Bowl during the Great Depression. Guthrie wrote several songs about this grim event, including "Dust Storm Disaster" and "So Long, It's Been Good to Know Yuh." The lyrics to both songs are reprinted below.

Dust Storm Disaster
(The Great Dust Storm)

On the fourteenth day of April of nineteen thirty five
There struck the worst of dust storms that ever filled the sky.
You could see that dust storm comin', the cloud looked deathlike black,
And through our mighty nation it left a dreadful track.

From Oklahoma City to the Arizona line
Dakota and Nebraska to the lazy Rio Grande.
It fell across our city like a curtain of black rolled down
We thought it was our judgment we thought it was our doom.

The radio reported we listened with alarm
The wild and windy actions of this great mysterious storm.
From Albuquerque and Clovis and all New Mexico
They said it was the blackest that ever they had saw.

In old Dodge City, Kansas, the dust had rung their knell,
And a few more comrades sleeping on top of old Boot Hill.
From Denver, Colorado, they said it blew so strong,

They thought that they could hold out, but they didn't know how long.

Our relatives were huddled into their oil boom shacks,
And the children they were crying as it whistled through the cracks.
And the family was crowded into their little room,
They thought the world had ended, and they thought it was their doom.

The storm took place at sundown, it lasted through the night,
When we looked out next morning, we saw a terrible sight.
We saw outside our window where wheatfields they had grown,
Was now a rippling ocean of dust the wind had blown.

It covered up our fences, it covered up our barns,
It covered up our tractors in this wild and dusty storm.
We loaded our jalopies and piled our families in,
We rattled down that highway to never come back again.

So Long, It's Been Good To Know Yuh (Dusty Old Dust)

I've sung this song, but I'll sing it again,
Of the place that I lived on the wild windy plains,
In the month called April, county called Gray,
And here's what all of the people there say:

[chorus]
So long, it's been good to know ye,
So long, it's been good to know ye,
So long, it's been good to know ye,
This dusty old dust is a-getting my home,
And I've got to be drifting along.

A dust storm hit, and it hit like thunder;
It dusted us over, and it covered us under;
Blocked out the traffic and blocked out the sun,
Straight for home all the people did run.
Singin': [chorus]

We talked of the end of the world, and then
We'd sing a song and then sing it again;
We'd sit for an hour and not say a word,
And then these words would be heard: [chorus]

The sweethearts sat in the dark and sparked,
They hugged and kissed in that dusty old dark.
They sighed and cried, hugged and kissed,
Instead of marriage, they talked like this:
"Honey ..." [chorus]

Now, the telephone rang, and it jumped off the wall,
That was the preacher a-making his call.
He said, "Kind friend, this may be the end;
You've got your last chance of salvation of sin."

The churches was jammed, and the churches was packed,
And that dusty old dust storm blowed so black;
Preacher could not read a word of his text;
And he folded his specs, and he took up collection,
Said: [chorus]

Source: Guthrie, Woody. "Dust Storm Disaster" and "So Long It's Been Good to Know Yuh," The Richmond Organization/Folkways Music. Available online at http://www.woody guthrie.org/Lyrics/.

Remembering "Black Sunday"

In 1931 an extended drought settled over America's Great Plains. This drought, combined with years of careless farming practices, created terrible dust storms in subsequent years. By 1934 and 1935 conditions had become so dreadful in parts of Kansas, Oklahoma, Colorado, Texas, and New Mexico that thousands of farming families simply fled the region, which became known as the Dust Bowl. The worst of the storms of this grim period in American history took place on April 14, 1935. This "Black Sunday" storm terrorized towns and farms across a large swath of the Great Plains. The following is an account of the Black Sunday storm from Harley Holladay, who was thirteen years old when the storm rolled over his family's farm outside of Dodge City, Kansas.

It was such a nice clear Sunday. We had hung the laundry out on the line that morning, and mother had washed the upholstered chairs and set them out to dry. I walked up to our horse pond and had picked up a stone to skip across the water. While I was throwing I happened to look up and noticed this long gray line on the horizon. It looked like a thunderhead, but it was too long and flat and it was rolling toward me way too fast. I sprinted to the house to tell my parents that the dust was coming but they wouldn't believe it until they went outside and looked for themselves. Then we started hauling in clothes as fast as we could, just snatching them in armloads and running. The cloud caught me outside with a load of clothes. I couldn't see anything at all. It was black as night. I got down on my hands and knees and tried to crawl toward the house. I finally felt the porch, and reached up and opened the screen door and crawled inside.

For a long time it was total blackness inside, except for one thing. When I looked out the window I could see our radio antenna outlined in static electricity. There were little balls of fire all over it caused by dirt particles rubbing together. It was spooky. Finally the sun began to shine as a faint glow of orange light coming in through the windows. As it got lighter, I could see baskets and brush sailing past us. It felt like we were flying through space.

[When the storm was over they stepped outside. Dust was heaped in the yard like sand dunes in a desert. Cattle and farm equipment were buried. Jackrabbits loped through the dunes. As always, Harley and his family cleared their throats and dug out.]

"Harley Holladay: Black Sunday" from *We Were There Too! Young People in U.S. History* by Phillip Hoose. Copyright © 2001 Phillip Hoose. Reprinted by permission of Farrar, Strauss, and Giroux, LLC.

I guess we had gotten used to it, because it had been that way for a long time. Our windows were taped up and the cracks in our walls were stuffed but nothing kept the dust out. Whenever we ate a meal we had to turn our plates and cups and glasses over until the exact time the meal was served. Even then, you could write your name in dust on your glass by the time the meal was done. Every night before we went to bed we scooped a little water into our noses and blew out the dirt. We put covers over our faces and a sheet over my little sister's crib. Some people slept with masks on.

You didn't want to get caught out in a storm, either. Some families strung clothesline between the house and the barn so that they could always find their way back to the house. We always made sure we had food and water with us when we left the house. When the dust started flying and I was away from the home I tried to find a fenceline to follow. My father used my brother and I as guides when he was plowing with the tractor in the fields. I'd stand at one end of the field with a kerosene light and my brother would shine a light at the other end. My dad would try to drive straight between us. The dust came so fast that it would cover up the tractor's tracks.

I was in World War II when the rain came back to Kansas, but I was still thinking a lot about the farm. One night in Italy I had the most wonderful dream. I was back on the farm in Kansas and we were having a rainshower at last. It was a big, loud thunderstorm, with buckets of rain just soaking the ground. I was so happy. And then someone was shaking me awake and there were tracer bullets and anti-aircraft fire all around. We were under attack. But in my dream the thunder of gunfire was a great blessing. That's how much rain meant to a Dust Bowl boy.

Source: Holladay, Harley, interview with Phillip Hoose. *We Were There, Too! Young People in U.S. History.* New York: Farrar Straus Giroux, 2001.

Battling the Dust Bowl and Rural Poverty

The Dust Bowl conditions that afflicted the Great Plains during the mid-1930s sparked a swift response from the Roosevelt administration. It approved major new reforms and programs to address the flawed farming practices that contributed to the Dust Bowl and to provide economic help to poor farmers all across the country. This federal effort was spearheaded by Henry Wallace, who was Roosevelt's secretary of agriculture, and Hugh Hammond Bennett, chief of the Agriculture Department's Soil Conservation Service. The following excerpts are from testimony that Bennett delivered on March 9, 1938, to a Special Senate Committee to Investigate Unemployment and Relief. Bennett emphasizes that rural poverty and soil erosion are closely linked and have to be treated together.

Soil erosion is a serious cause of rural impoverishment. To the nation as a whole, uncontrolled erosion has brought a gradual and continuing reduction of productive agricultural land. Estimates based on a reconnaissance erosion survey of the United States, made in 1935, show that approximately 50 million acres of once productive agricultural land has been virtually ruined for further cultivation. Most of this area has been abandoned, although an occasional farmer hangs on to patches left between gullies. Another 50 million acres is in about as bad condition, but the severely eroded areas are intermingled with patches of better land, so that abandonment has not been so nearly complete. On the latter, considerably more impoverished agriculture is continuing. From a second 100 million acres a large part or all of the topsoil has washed off, and on this many thousands of farmers struggle for a meager living. Erosion is getting actively under way on still another vast area, aggregating something over 100 million acres, and will continue its depredations if agricultural practices are not altered to check the process of land wastage.

To the individual farmer erosion brings increased costs, lowered productivity, and on many farms outright ruin of the land, piece by piece, until frequently, abandonment of entire fields or the whole farm is forced. Erosion is not confined to the poorer and economically sub-marginal farms, but its incidence is greater and its effect most serious in the economically distressed areas of the country. An examination of the land of the United States classed as economically sub-marginal shows that most of it is physically poor land, either originally or as the result of erosion. Economic factors, such as low prices, reduced markets, or agricultural surpluses, are perhaps the most serious immediate causes of rural economic distress, but in the long run soil wastage is the most certain cause of permanent agricultural impoverishment. Even in times of great agricultural prosperity, land destroyed by erosion will fail to support a prosperous agriculture. Moreover, a subsistence type of agriculture relatively little affected by the fluctuations of the economic cycle is impossible on land riddled by gullies or stripped to stubborn clay subsoil or to bedrock by continuing sheet erosion....

The results of an applied program of erosion control, taken from a large number of demonstration projects in various distinctive problem areas throughout the country, will illustrate the relation of this kind of work to the alleviation of rural difficulties cause by excessive soil erosion.

A demonstration of soil and water conservation was started by the Soil Conservation Service late in 1935 on the watershed of Pecan Creek, near Muskogee, Oklahoma. Cooperative work has been carried out on 203 of the 268 farms in the watershed. Of these, approximately 70 percent were tenants or share-croppers, most of them operating on the basis of one-year arrangements with their landlords. Every year, between cropping seasons, many of the tenants were in the habit of moving to some other farm, for a new start in life. Erosion was very severe on most of the farms, and serious on all of them. Prevailing farm practices were such that the evil was spreading at a progressively increasing rate. Fields and parts of fields were being abandoned to an increasing extent every year. Most of the land was definitely on the way out, insofar as further crop use was concerned.

After two years of cooperative soil and water conservation work, soil washing has been largely controlled with practical farm measures, which at the same time have caused much of the rainfall that formerly ran to waste immediately after every rain of any importance to be stored in the reservoir of the soil for use by crops during dry summer periods.

Better yields are being obtained—more production per acre—as the result of water conservation and stabilization of sloping land, by reason of the introduction of crop rotations, contour cultivation and strip cropping; by the building of protective field terraces and waterways safeguarded with grass; and by closing gullies and retiring highly erodible steep lands to the permanent protection of grass or trees.

All of the farmers with whom the Service has cooperated in Pecan Creek Watershed now have 5-year cooperative working arrangements, under which it has been agreed that the protective installations, and soil-building and water-conserving practices will be carefully maintained over a period of five years. These agreements have been made with the approval of the landlords and have had the effect in many cases of changing the term of tenancy from a one-year to a five-year basis.

Thus, many operators who were moving from farm to farm every year, without getting anywhere on the economic ladder, now have at least the opportunity of a longer stay on a given tract of land. Actually, as well as can be determined, both tenant and landlords are pleased with this new situation of land safe-guarded from the ravages of erosion and excessive loss of rainfall. Annual moving of families has practically ceased; outside tenants are trying to rent land within the project area. Apparently, both landlord and tenant have come to see increased opportunity and security in this new type of agriculture, with its better yields and protected land. They have come to a better understanding, and many landowners are telling their tenants they can remain where they are so long as they go ahead with these new and helpful practices. A greater love for the land has sprung up in that community, and a consciousness of man's responsibility to defend the soil he tills against the destructive effects of erosion.

Economically, both landlord and tenant have been materially helped, and it is significant that the stability and security given the land of the area have given an increased measure of stability and security to the farm population of the area.

In some parts of the United States the problem of rural distress is more acute. Perhaps there is no extensive area in which the problem is more widespread than in the wind-erosion region of the Great Plains. In that vast area, extending from the Panhandle of Texas to the Canadian border, about 70 percent of the land is affected in some degree by wind or water erosion, and approximately a quarter of the area is affected severely. Social and economic problems of the greatest seriousness exist through the region. Despite the fact that thousands of farm families have left the area in recent years the Federal Government is reported to have spent more than $130,000,000 in various forms of work and drought relief in the Great Plains counties in the three years from April, 1933, to April, 1936.

As the report of the Great Plains Committee points out, conditions in the plains are the result of a complex of physical, economic, and cultural factors which must be taken into account in solving this problem. I think it is evident, however, that the problem of soil erosion—particularly by wind—as well as that of water conservation, must be solved if the agriculture of the Great Plains is to be economically stable and secure. Moreover, the experience of the Soil Conservation Service in its erosion-control demonstration projects indicates that those practices necessary to prevent wind erosion at the same time contribute to the solution of many of the economic problems of the region....

Erosion may be a result as well as an important cause of rural impoverishment, for farmers may be forced by economic circumstances to disregard the need for soil conservation and to farm their lands exploitatively for as long as they can be made to last under such practice. The impoverished farmer on impoverished land may not have the resources to stop the erosion on his land. He frequently has only a small tract of land and his holding is usually located within some critical erosion area, such as the steeper portion of a watershed. Because the land is poor the farmer is driven to greater efforts to force from it what livelihood he can. This, in turn, further impoverishes what little land is left. Thus, intensive cultivation of sloping land without proper erosion control accentuates both the erosion problem and the relief problem. The poor farmer on poor land frequently is unable, without assistance, to check an impoverishing process which drives both himself and his land from worse to worse. Even in comparatively prosperous communities the occasional poor farmer stands as a special obstacle to adequate soil conservation in the community.

It is on steep land that water erosion usually gets out of control most rapidly, to ruin not only that farm but to damage lower slopes, to cover neighboring valley lands with unproductive sand or clay, and to fill stream channels with the products of wasted land. Where the land is steep, poor, and of complicated topography, the per acre cost of erosion control is far greater than on a comparable downstream area of smoother surface features. Thus, even if all farmers were possessed of equal funds per acre of holdings, the operator on steep land would be at a relative disadvantage in paying for the installation and maintenance of measures and practices necessary for controlling erosion, because of the physical disadvantages of his land. In humid regions, it is on the steeper uplands as a rule that the poorest farmers are concentrated. Where wind erosion is the principal menace, topography is not an important factor, the poorer farmers being located on lands which too generally have been bared of vegetation. Hence, on lands where the need for controlling erosion is most imperative, where the danger to the countryside is greatest, and the cost of control highest, we find poverty preventing a recognition of the need for soil conservation; we see a desperate struggle to wrest a livelihood from eroding hillsides intensifying the danger of downstream damage; and we discover an impoverished citizenry which, irrespective of how keenly it may sense the danger or wish to correct it, is economically unable to do so.

If our erosion control program is made adaptable to such small holdings and to persons without means, or with inadequate means, by permitting greater Federal contributions to impoverished farmers, such unfortunate operators may be able to continue on a subsistence basis without being forced onto relief. Conversely, if sufficient relief should be provided, it is possible that such individuals might be able to contribute enough to the current erosion-control program to check the loss of their soil and eventually to emerge as self-sustaining subsistence units. If assistance is provided neither from an erosion-control program, nor from relief sources, it is difficult to see how such individuals and their land can avoid progressive deterioration.

In addition to this large class of "relief" or "submarginal" farmers who find themselves in a position to do little or nothing either for their land or themselves, there is probably a larger group which, due to a combination of erosion, soil exhaustion, and adverse economic factors (as low prices) is progressively approaching this meager subsistence level. An adequate program for this group is important because if nothing is done to arrest their declining economy they, themselves, will soon descend to a relief status, and further costs for relief and rehabilitation, otherwise preventable may have to be assumed.

The connection between rural relief and soil erosion cannot, however, be considered exclusively in terms of individual cases. The problem exists on an area-wide basis. Thus, there is a recognizable degree of correlation between critical erosion areas and areas where the bulk of the farmers are on a marginal or near-subsistence basis. The assumption that farmers of a community are essentially able to control erosion themselves if correctly advised and organized may in some instances overlook the economics of the locality. Where the bulk of a community consists of impoverished farmers on eroding soil, as is true over a large part of such extensive areas as the Appalachian highlands, the middle and upper Rio Grande watershed, and drought and dust stricken portions of the Great Plains, assistance for the correction or arrest of this condition must be sought outside, as well as inside, the community involved. If adequate steps are not taken to better these situations, the passage of time can only witness a progressive intensification of such unfavorable situations, both for the land and for the people on the land.

Any consideration of the connection between rural poverty and soil erosion should not overlook the possibilities of erosion-control programs being carried out by the rural relief workers themselves. Our experience over a period of four years has shown conclusively that soil conservation work can well be adapted to relief programs. Including CCC camps engaged in erosion work, the Soil Conservation Service at one time was employing over 123,000 persons on a relief status. Today, the Service is still furnishing employment to more than 70,000, largely in CCC work. Erosion-control work requires largely unskilled labor and is a relatively inexpensive form of work relief (current average man-year cost is $696). It provides a type of work which rural relief persons can recognize as being of immediate benefit to themselves, their neighbors, and the community, and it is work for which they have had considerable training. From the standpoint of administration of relief, if supplies projects in areas where other work programs are difficult too organize or supervise. Indeed, it is one of the few programs in which the relief work itself is carried on in sparsely populated and impoverished regions where so many rural relief cases are found.

Specifically, in December, 1935, the Soil Conservation Service was employing from relief funds more than 32,000 workers (not including CCC enrollees) on erosion-control demonstration and work projects. These men were engaged in such outdoor tasks as:

> Tree and shrub planting, together with seeding and other improvements, on depleted pastures and steep cultivated fields retired from cultivation to permanent stability as woodland, wildlife, and pasture areas;
>
> Building field terraces and diversion waterways;
>
> Sodding the outlets of such water-control channels;
>
> Constructing check-dams of brush, rock, or concrete;
>
> Building stock-water reservoirs;
>
> Building dikes for diverting water running to waste along expanding gullies, for cheap irrigation;
>
> Laying out lines for contour cultivation and strip cropping;
>
> Relocating fences;
>
> Re-sodding worn-out fields for protection or for permanent pasture.

From a beginning, in August, 1935, when no labor of this kind was employed, the Service developed its relief labor program at the rate of a thousand new workers a week, until by December of that year the organization was the first of all the Federal agencies to reach the quota set for it by the WPA; and for a long time thereafter it employed a larger number of workers than many agencies which had larger emergency allotments. This was partly due to a helpful spirit of enthusiasm in getting the program started, but primarily to the fact that soil-conservation operations require relatively little expensive equipment. Once technical supervisors are available, a great number of unskilled and semi-skilled persons can be furnished quick employment on work of permanent public value, in those communities prepared to provide the necessary limited cooperation.

An example of the speed with which relief persons may be employed on a soil and water-conservation program is illustrated by the Service's experience in the fall of 1936 with drought relief. Covering a space of four and a half months the Soil Conservation Service expended approximately $2,200,000 in furnishing employment too about 10,000 drought-stricken farmers in twenty states. In Colorado, however, money was not made available until November 12. There, the technical staff was gathered together, a program developed, tasks assigned, and supervisors sent to their respective field stations to select their drought-relief areas. On November 19, just one week later, the first stock-water dam was started.

This money remained available for six weeks only, but during that time 137 greatly needed dams were constructed at advantageous points, and employment was furnished to 679 needy persons. The wide distribution of this work demonstrated the value of water-conserving dams and soil-conserving methods to almost every problem area through the Plains section of the State, and greatly increased interest in practical erosion control. Work, most of it construction of dams for impounding water supplies, was only engaged in with cooperators who were willing to sign the customary five-year working plan agreement of the Service, which provides for the application of an integrated erosion-control program for an entire farm or ranch.

These cooperators continue to furnish the Service with yearly reports on the performance of these dams, and the field staff keeps in touch with them to encourage them to carry the farm or ranch program to completion. The farmers and ranchmen have carried on splendidly; they have written many letters describing their appreciation of the benefits this work has brought them. Local public opinion is said to consider this type of work as being almost universally satisfactory, not only to farmers and ranchmen but to the general public of the drought stricken area. Experience has shown that where the relief workers were actually farmers, and where they were engaged in constructing dams and other drought relief and erosion-control operations on farms of their own community, the enthusiasm was such that, with the training acquired through actual work, a number of them continued to install similar structures cooperatively on each other's farms after the paid program was over.

The Soil Conservation Service was set up by Congress primarily to demonstrate to the farmers of the country how soil erosion could be controlled or prevented. This necessitated the carrying out of an extensive field operations program, and it was in this program that relief workers were found to be so useful. In any extension of conservation operations, as there must be if the Nation's soil is to be conserved, opportunities can be provided for important utilization of rural relief labor. In this connection, it should be pointed out that a number of soil conservation districts have been formed as legal subdivisions of states. Many of these districts will need all possible assistance including labor to establish effective control measures under an applicable, organized plan, and with the technical aid of these agencies equipped for such service.

The matters to which I have referred give some indication of what has been and what can be done to mitigate the impoverishing effects of erosion, both on the land and on the rural population. A final observation with respect to the relationship between soil erosion and rural human impoverishment is that, if left alone, the one accentuates the other, where as if proper steps are taken the amelioration of either provides a basis for the curbing of both.

Source: Testimony of H.H. Bennett, March 4, 1938, before the Special Senate Committee to Investigate Unemployment and Relief. Available online at U.S. Department of Agriculture, Natural Resources Conservation Service, "Speeches of Hugh Hammond Bennett," http://www.nrcs.usda.gov/about/history/speeches/19380309.html.

Roosevelt Unveils the Second New Deal

In the spring of 1935 President Franklin D. Roosevelt launched an ambitious new set of federal programs and initiatives to restore the United States to good economic health. Since his first round of reforms were widely known as the New Deal, his 1935 proposals came to be termed the Second New Deal.

On April 28, 1935, Roosevelt delivered one of his famous "fireside chats" to the nation to explain the cornerstones of the Second New Deal. He spent most of this radio address on three subjects: Social Security legislation, the creation of the Works Progress Administration, and his desire to see Congress renew the 1933 National Industrial Recovery Act. This act was actually declared unconstitutional one month later by the U.S. Supreme Court, to Roosevelt's great disappointment. But the Social Security Act and the Works Progress Administration were among the greatest achievements of his presidency. Following is the text of his April 28 broadcast:

Since my annual message to the Congress on January fourth, last, I have not addressed the general public over the air. In the many weeks since that time the Congress has devoted itself to the arduous task of formulating legislation necessary to the country's welfare. It has made and is making distinct progress.

Before I come to any of the specific measures, however, I want to leave in your minds one clear fact. The Administration and the Congress are not proceeding in any haphazard fashion in this task of government. Each of our steps has a definite relationship to every other step. The job of creating a program for the Nation's welfare is, in some respects, like the building of a ship. At different points on the coast where I often visit they build great seagoing ships. When one of these ships is under construction and the steel frames have been set in the keel, it is difficult for a person who does not know ships to tell how it will finally look when it is sailing the high seas.

It may seem confused to some, but out of the multitude of detailed parts that go into the making of the structure the creation of a useful instrument for man ultimately comes. It is that way with the making of a national policy. The objective of the Nation has greatly changed in three years. Before that time individual self-interest and group selfishness were paramount in public thinking. The general good was at a discount.

Three years of hard thinking have changed the picture. More and more people, because of clearer thinking and a better understanding, are considering the whole rather than a mere part relating to one section or to one crop, or to one industry, or to an individual private occupation. That is a tremendous gain for the principles of democracy. The overwhelming majority of people in this country know how to sift the wheat from the chaff in what they hear and what they read. They know that the process of the constructive rebuilding of America cannot be done in a day or a year, but that it is being done in spite of the few who seek to confuse them and to profit by their confusion. Americans as a whole are feeling a lot better—a lot more cheerful than for many, many years.

The most difficult place in the world to get a clear open perspective of the country as a whole is Washington. I am reminded sometimes of what President Wilson once said: "So many people come to Washington who know things that are not so, and so few people who know anything about what the people of the United States are thinking about." That is why I occasionally leave this scene of action for a few days to go fishing or back home to Hyde Park, so that I can have a chance to think quietly about the country as a whole. "To get away from the trees," as they say, "and to look at the whole forest." This duty of seeing the country in a long-range perspective is one which, in a very special manner, attaches to this office to which you have chosen me. Did you ever stop to think that there are, after all, only two positions in the Nation that are filled by the vote of all of the voters—the President and the Vice-President? That makes it particularly necessary for the Vice-President and for me to conceive of our duty toward the entire country. I speak, therefore, tonight, to and of the American people as a whole.

My most immediate concern is in carrying out the purposes of the great work program just enacted by the Congress. Its first objective is to put men and women now on the relief rolls to work and, incidentally, to assist materially in our already unmistakable march toward recovery. I shall not confuse my discussion by a multitude of figures. So many figures are quoted to prove so many things. Sometimes it depends upon what paper you read and what broadcast you hear. Therefore, let us keep our minds on two or three simple, essential facts in connection with this problem of unemployment.

It is true that while business and industry are definitely better our relief rolls are still too large. However, for the first time in five years the relief rolls have declined instead of increased during the winter months. They are still declining. The simple fact is that many million more people have private work today than two years ago today or one year ago today, and every day that passes offers more chances to work for those who want to work. In spite of the fact that unemployment remains a serious problem here as in every other nation, we have come to recognize the possibility and the necessity of certain helpful remedial measures. These measures are of two kinds. The first is to make provisions intended to relieve, to minimize, and to prevent future unemployment; the second is to establish the practical means to help those who are unemployed in this present emergency. Our social security legislation is an attempt to answer the first of these questions. Our work relief program the second.

The program for social security now pending before the Congress is a necessary part of the future unemployment policy of the government. While our present and projected expenditures for work relief are wholly within the reasonable limits of our national credit resources, it is obvious that we cannot continue to create governmental deficits for that purpose year after year. We must begin now to make provision for the future. That is why our social security program is an important part of the complete picture. It proposes, by means of old age pensions, to help those who have reached the age of retirement to give up their jobs and thus give to the younger generation greater opportunities for work and to give to all a feeling of security as they look toward old age.

The unemployment insurance part of the legislation will not only help to guard the individual in future periods of lay-off against dependence upon relief, but it will, by sustaining purchasing power, cushion the shock of economic distress. Another helpful feature of unemployment insurance is the incentive it will give to employers to plan more carefully in order that unemployment may be prevented by the stabilizing of employment itself.

Provisions for social security, however, are protections for the future. Our responsibility for the immediate necessities of the unemployed has been met by the Congress through the most comprehensive work plan in the history of the Nation. Our problem is to put to work three and one-half million employable persons now on the relief rolls. It is a problem quite as much for private industry as for the government.

We are losing no time getting the government's vast work relief program underway, and we have every reason to believe that it should be in full swing by autumn. In directing it, I shall recognize six fundamental principles:

(1) The projects should be useful.

(2) Projects shall be of a nature that a considerable proportion of the money spent will go into wages for labor.

(3) Projects which promise ultimate return to the Federal Treasury of a considerable proportion of the costs will be sought.

(4) Funds allotted for each project should be actually and promptly spent and not held over until later years.

(5) In all cases projects must be of a character to give employment to those on the relief rolls.

(6) Projects will be allocated to localities or relief areas in relation to the number of workers on relief rolls in those areas.

I next want to make it clear exactly how we shall direct the work.

(1) I have set up a Division of Applications and Information to which all proposals for the expenditure of money must go for preliminary study and consideration.

(2) After the Division of Applications and Information has sifted those projects, they will be sent to an Allotment Division composed of representatives of the more important governmental agencies charged with carrying on work relief projects. The group will also include representatives of cities, and of labor, farming, banking and industry. This Allotment Division will consider all of the recommendations submitted to it and such projects as they approve will be next submitted to the President who under the Act is required to make final allocations.

(3) The next step will be to notify the proper government agency in whose field the project falls, and also to notify another agency which I am creating—a Progress Division. This Division will have the duty of coordinating the purchases of materials and supplies and of making certain that people who are employed will be taken from the relief rolls. It will also have the responsibility of determining work payments in various localities, of making full use of existing employment services and to assist people engaged in relief work to move as rapidly as possible back into private employment when such employment is available. Moreover, this Division will be charged with keeping projects moving on schedule.

(4) I have felt it to be essentially wise and prudent to avoid, so far as possible, the creation of new governmental machinery for supervising this

work. The National Government now has at least sixty different agencies with the staff and the experience and the competence necessary to carry on the two hundred and fifty or three hundred kinds of work that will be undertaken. These agencies, therefore, will simply be doing on a somewhat enlarged scale the same sort of things that they have been doing. This will make certain that the largest possible portion of the funds allotted will be spent for actually creating new work and not for building up expensive overhead organizations here in Washington.

For many months preparations have been under way. The allotment of funds for desirable projects has already begun. The key men for the major responsibilities of this great task already have been selected. I well realize that the country is expecting before this year is out to see the "dirt fly," as they say, in carrying on the work, and I assure my fellow citizens that no energy will be spared in using these funds effectively to make a major attack upon the problem of unemployment.

Our responsibility is to all of the people in this country. This is a great national crusade to destroy enforced idleness which is an enemy of the human spirit generated by this depression. Our attack upon these enemies must be without stint and without discrimination. No sectional, no political distinctions can be permitted.

It must, however, be recognized that when an enterprise of this character is extended over more than three thousand counties throughout the Nation, there may be occasional instances of inefficiency, bad management, or misuse of funds. When cases of this kind occur, there will be those, of course, who will try to tell you that the exceptional failure is characteristic of the entire endeavor. It should be remembered that in every big job there are some imperfections. There are chiselers in every walk of life; there are those in every industry who are guilty of unfair practices, every profession has its black sheep, but long experience in government has taught me that the exceptional instances of wrong-doing in government are probably less numerous than in almost every other line of endeavor.

The most effective means of preventing such evils in this work relief program will be the eternal vigilance of the American people themselves. I call upon my fellow citizens everywhere to cooperate with me in making this the most efficient and the cleanest example of public enterprise the world has ever seen. It is time to provide a smashing answer for those cynical men who say that a democracy cannot be honest and efficient. If you will help, this can be done. I, therefore, hope you will watch the work in every corner of this Nation. Feel free to criticize. Tell me of instances where work can be done better, or where improper practices prevail. Neither you nor I want criticism conceived in a purely fault-finding or partisan spirit, but I am jealous of the right of every citizen to call to the attention of his or her government examples of how the public money can be more effectively spent for the benefit of the American people.

I now come, my friends, to a part of the remaining business before the Congress. It has under consideration many measures which provide for the rounding out of the program of economic and social reconstruction with which we have been concerned for two years. I can mention only a few of them tonight, but I do not want my mention of specific measures to be interpreted as lack of interest in or disapproval of many other important proposals that are pending.

The National Industrial Recovery Act expires on the sixteenth of June. After careful consideration, I have asked the Congress to extend the life of this useful agency of government. As we have proceeded with the administration of this Act, we have found from time to time more and more useful ways of promoting its purposes. No reasonable person wants to abandon our present gains—we must continue to protect children, to enforce minimum wages, to prevent excessive hours, to safeguard, define and enforce collective bargaining, and, while retaining fair competition, to eliminate so far as humanly possible, the kinds of unfair practices by selfish minorities which unfortunately did more than anything else to bring about the recent collapse of industries. There is likewise pending before the Congress legislation to provide for the elimination of unnecessary holding companies in the public utility field.

I consider this legislation a positive recovery measure. Power production in this country is virtually back to the 1929 peak. The operating companies in the gas and electric utility field are by and large in good condition. But under holding company domination the utility industry has long been hopelessly at war within itself and with public sentiment. By far the greater part of the general decline in utility securities had occurred before I was inaugurated. The absentee management of unnecessary holding company control has lost touch with and has lost the sympathy of the communities it pretends to serve. Even more significantly, it has given the country as a whole an uneasy apprehension of overconcentrated economic power.

A business that loses the confidence of its customers and the good will of the public cannot long continue to be a good risk for the investor. This legislation will serve the investor by ending the conditions which have caused that lack of confidence and good will. It will put the public utility operating industry on a sound basis for the future, both in its public relations and in its internal relations.

This legislation will not only in the long run result in providing lower electric and gas rates to the consumer, but it will protect the actual value and earning power of properties now owned by thousands of investors who have little protection under the old laws against what used to be called frenzied finance. It will not destroy values.

Not only business recovery, but the general economic recovery of the Nation will be greatly stimulated by the enactment of legislation designed to improve the status of our transportation agencies. There is need for legislation providing for the regulation of interstate transportation by buses and trucks, to regulate transportation by water, new provisions for strengthening our Merchant Marine and air transport, measures for the strengthening of the Interstate Commerce Commission to enable it to carry out a rounded conception of the national transportation system in which the benefits of private ownership are retained, while the public stake in these important services is protected by the public's government.

Finally, the reestablishment of public confidence in the banks of the Nation is one of the most hopeful results of our efforts as a Nation to reestablish public confidence in private banking. We all know that private banking actually exists by virtue of the permission of and regulation by the people as a whole, speaking through their government. Wise public policy, however, requires not only that banking be safe but that its resources be most fully utilized, in the economic life of the country. To this end it was decided more than twenty years ago that the government should assume the responsibility of providing a means by which the credit of the Nation might be controlled, not by a few private banking institutions, but by a body with public prestige and authority. The answer to this demand was the Federal Reserve System. Twenty years of experience with this system have justified the efforts made to create it, but these twenty years have shown by experience definite possibilities for improvement. Certain proposals made to amend the Federal Reserve Act deserve prompt and favorable action by the Congress. They are a minimum of wise readjustment of our Federal Reserve system in the light of past experience and present needs.

These measures I have mentioned are, in large part, the program which under my constitutional duty I have recommended to the Congress. They are essential factors in a rounded program for national recovery. They contemplate the enrichment of our national life by a sound and rational ordering of its various elements and wise provisions for the protection of the weak against the strong. Never since my inauguration in March, 1933, have I felt so unmistakably the atmosphere of recovery. But it is more than the recovery of the material basis of our individual lives. It is the recovery of confidence in our democratic processes and institutions. We have survived all of the arduous burdens and the threatening dangers of a great economic calamity. We have in the darkest moments of our national trials retained our faith in our own ability to master our destiny. Fear is vanishing and confidence is growing on every side, renewed faith in the vast possibilities of human beings to improve their material and spiritual status through the instrumentality of the democratic form of government. That faith is receiving its just reward. For that we can be thankful to the God who watches over America.

Source: John T. Woolley and Gerhard Peters, *The American Presidency Project* [online]. Santa Barbara, CA: University of California (hosted), Gerhard Peters (database). Available online at http://www.presidency.ucsb.edu/ws/?pid=15046.

The *Saturday Evening Post* Condemns Roosevelt and the New Deal

During the Great Depression, many conservative business interests, newspaper editors, and ordinary citizens expressed doubts about Roosevelt's leadership and alarm about his New Deal reforms. Some of these objections were based on self-interest, but others stemmed from genuine concerns about the future welfare of the United States. The following editorial was published on November 7, 1936, by the editors of the Saturday Evening Post, *one of the nation's most popular magazines. It summarizes many of the concerns voiced by Roosevelt's political opponents. The editorial also offers a positive assessment of Republican Alf Landon, who was Roosevelt's opponent in the 1936 presidential election.*

"Pride and Prejudice"

People who are moved almost wholly by their emotions, prejudices, passions and pride of party, who are stirred to unreasoning anger by the presentation of any side of the questions before the country except their side, are always quick to accuse their opponents of blind partisanship. They demand that all newspapers and periodicals, except those that reflect their own views, be neutral, as they call it. They are quick to resent criticisms of propaganda handouts by press agents who are paid out of taxation, or strictures on the subsidizing of special classes by the New Deal.

In a period like this, when the American System—and that means much more than the business system—is at stake, it is important to have close scrutiny and free criticism of the plans and policies of those in power. Being neutral in thought or in speech is just another name for indifference, spinelessness or cowardice.

As far as THE SATURDAY EVENING POST is concerned, the personalities of the candidates are unimportant, except as they have a direct bearing on the ideas for which they stand. We have no doubt, as his intimates claim, that the President has a charming personality and that Governor Landon is less winning in his manner and of a more homespun personality. We all know that the President can sing like a canary over the radio, or swoop down like a hawk on the alleged "economic royalists" in a speech. We all know that Governor Landon is not a sweet singer over the radio or given to vituperation of any class in his speeches. He seems to regard Americans, not as antagonistic classes, seething with hatred of one another, but as one people.

The matter of first importance in the case of the candidates is the ideas for which they stand, for they are not so much personalities as symbols of ideas and promises. Once in the presidential office, these ideas and promises become concrete in action or lack of action. Candidate Landon has not yet been tested in the presidential office. Candidate Roosevelt has been. And it is because of his record as President that we view the possibility of four years more of the New Deal with misgivings.

If Candidate Roosevelt, as President, had stood on the Democratic platform and steered his course by his pre-election promises, instead of throwing both overboard, and even if, for a sound reason, he had temporarily gone about on a new tack, we should have had no criticism to offer, just as we offered no criticism of President [Woodrow] Wilson—whose re-election we advocated—until he went abroad and agreed to the Treaty of Versailles. So, when President Roosevelt began to look askance at the Constitution, and to set up new instruments of power, which, he frankly confessed, might be dangerous in the hands of another man, we felt it was impossible to follow him, for we believe that his new instruments of power are dangerous in his hands.

THE SATURDAY EVENING POST, owing to its large edition and its world-wide circulation, must go to press several weeks before it is distributed to subscribers and buyers from the newsstands, so we shall not be able to comment on the election before the last of November.

But whether Landon or Roosevelt is elected, we shall continue to be nonpartisan, in the real sense of the word, and criticize the policies of either as President whenever we feel that they are unsound or unwise.

The Final Question

This year's presidential campaign has had all the outward marks of confusion and complexity. People have been perplexed, or bored, by the very number and variety of different issues. Charges and countercharges, claims and counterclaims, have followed one another in bewildering succession. To sift grains of truth from oceans of rumor, to pick out facts from the mass of allegations, has been almost impossible. Nor have party lines themselves been helpfully distinct and clear, as in the past; the usual allegiances have shifted too radically for that.

But the confusion is more seeming than real. After all, the voter must ask himself the final question, which is whether, in his opinion, a continuance of Mr. Roosevelt's regime will tend to undermine the foundations, dissipate the substance and destroy the real spirit of the American system of representative government. Except in the mindset of extremists, there is no reason why necessary modifications might not be made in the form of that government. But Americans have got to decide whether the essential spirit of our system is in danger.

It is likely that the more extreme opponents of the New Deal and of its leader may have exaggerated, in the heat of the campaign, the extent of the discordant, disgruntled and radical elements which have come to Mr. Roosevelt's aid. There is no denying that his cause has an irresistible fascination for these groups, but in a country with more than seventy million potential voters and under a two-party system, either candidate is likely to have some embarrassing support.

No, the fundamental question is not whether Reds, for reasons of their own, favor Mr. Roosevelt's re-election, although such a fact can hardly be without significance. Nor is the underlying question whether his policies have retarded recovery. What the voter must finally decide in his own mind is whether the essential spirit and direction of the New Deal regime has been American or not.

It cannot be successfully denied that whatever the merits of New Deal policies, they have, as a whole, caused an appreciable drift away from individual responsibility and self-reliance. They have brought about an excessive, utterly fallacious and dangerous reliance upon government as a substitute for private endeavor and obligation. Worst of all, they have been based upon the juvenile assumption that social betterment does not need to be grown from the roots of character and moral suasion, but can be imposed from the head downwards at a single happy-go-lucky stroke, by compulsory legislation or by administrative decree.

These, in sober fact, are among the very essentials of New Deal policy, and no voter can escape the serious responsibility of deciding whether American institutions really fit into such a pattern.

The Sum of the Parts

There is always a tendency, especially in an election year, to distort and exaggerate the part which the President plays in our national picture. He is leader of his party, head of the Government, first citizen of the land, and in many respects the most powerful of earth's rulers. Nevertheless, it takes parts to make a whole; the President is only one, even if he is the most important part, and the whole is, after all, the sum of the parts. Thus it does not do at a time like this to consider only the election of President and Vice-President.

The extraordinary majority which the New Deal has had since 1932 in the House of Representatives has been, in the opinion of nearly all political observers, one of the chief causes of the excesses and follies of the New Deal. In other words, there has been no real check upon Executive whim. The President himself would have been better off if he had not been able to get everything he wanted. Ours is supposed to be a government of checks and balances, but because of this extraordinary Democratic majority in the House, one of the major checks on the Executive was lacking.

There is no implication in this statement that Republican congressmen are inherently better than Democratic; as a whole, the Republican minority in Congress has shown no remarkable traits of courage or altruism. But it is manifest to anyone who gives the subject a moment's thought that a more even division of power in the House of Representatives would at least promote discussion and thus check hasty legislation. As Congress comes back, as it is almost certain to do, to a more normal balance, there is hope that the winds of experiment gradually may be tempered.

But state as well as national issues should challenge the vigilance, in this election, of those citizens who have a respect for orderly representative government. The New Deal wave swept into power more than one governor and many local officials who, if we can believe stories in the press, act much as if they were pro-consuls in conquered territory. There have grown up, in many parts of the country, state and local political organizations which are consolidating their power by crude methods. Some of these officials have become such dictators that the citizens of their states actually fear them. In a few cases even intimidation does not seem to be too strong a weapon for these petty tyrants to use, and if their rule continues they may prove a real menace to freedom.

A careful observer and reporter of the American scene remarks that no matter how the present election comes out, the American people will not very long endure the Tammanyizing of America. This seems a bit unfair to the famous political organization, which has long been wise enough to practice a certain moderation in its conduct—a statement which apparently does not apply to the newer and somewhat similar organizations in other states. But, in any case, the welfare of the country demands that the aggrandizement of any state dictators be checked in this, and not in some future election.

Source: Editorial. *Saturday Evening Post,* November 7, 1936.

A Rabbi's Letter of Thanks to Roosevelt

Many of President Franklin D. Roosevelt's New Deal reforms were controversial, but most of them enjoyed the support of the majority of Americans. Poor and working-class Americans acknowledged that none of the president's Depression-fighting programs were perfect, but they kept millions of people afloat during the darkest days of the decade-long recession. This letter from a New York rabbi employed by the Works Progress Administration (WPA) reflects this viewpoint. The rabbi expresses some frustrations with inefficiencies within the WPA. Overall, though, he praises Roosevelt for his efforts on behalf of America's vulnerable citizens and assures the president that "the masses of the people are still with you."

Dear Mr. Roosevelt:

I have hesitated all this time to answer your letter of September 24, feeling that I probably did not come within the class of representative clergymen to whom it was addressed. I feel, however, that as one who has met all classes of the community, and one, who, from a long time back has been one of your sincerest supporters and well-wishers, I cannot deny the appeal so graciously expressed in your letter.

For about two years now I have been the supervisor of a project first in Work Relief and then under the Works Progress Administration. In addition during the last month I have acted as secretary to furnish free seats for a bureau conducted by Temple Emanuel and other congregations to furnish free seats for the Jewish holidays for those who could not afford to pay. This has brought me into direct contact with the very people for whom the Social Security Legislation and Works Program has been intended. I wish that those who are opposing such a program could meet these people. I could furnish instance after instance of old people who have worked hard all their lives, only to face desperate need in their old age; of middle-aged workers cast adrift not through their own incapability, but of those who employed them; of young people who have just completed their education and find that the working world has no place for them. I have found some shirkers and cheaters, but they are a very small minority; and the thing that has impressed me is the eagerness with which the unemployed seek for work, even the most difficult, in order that they may do their part in the community.

It goes then without question that I heartily applaud the work that the government has done in this direction and that I feel that it must continue as long as the necessity exists. I do not believe that government should assume full responsibility for employment—there is danger there. But as there is a social need which private business cannot or will not meet, it must be met by the American people as a whole, as a worth-while investment in its own citizens. While there is a distinct improvement in conditions as compared to the time when you assumed office, the emergency is still not over, and it particularly effects those classes who provide the luxury services of civilization and its intellectual achievements. Among the classes in which I find especial distress are the recent college graduates, both girls and boys, secretarial work, salesmen on commission, lawyers, clergymen, and artists.

As for the Works Program itself, I find that while it has been nobly conceived, it is often ineptly administered. Despite the fact that we have been called upon to make plans for a long time back and to elaborate on specifications, there is still great difficulty in fitting the right man to the job. I have sat for days at the central clearing offices, and know what I am talking about. Time after time I have been sent people who are absolutely disqualified for my work, just because no one else knows what to do with them; while on the other hand, those for whom I asked and whom I knew would be both serviceable to me and happy in the work are the very ones that I have been unable to obtain. At present I am feeling somewhat bitter since I am now seeing the project on which I have spent so much of my time and thought, which was designed especially for those who would be unemployable on anything else, which will benefit millions of people in the present and the future, and has won the highest praise from every official who has had anything to do with it, being thrown to the lions at the whim of a local committee, without having had the opportunity to defend itself or to explain its purpose. I realize that in so large an undertaking it is not always possible to secure ideal results, and perhaps I should not criticize at all, seeing that my general judgment on the program is that, while not entirely efficient, it is probably the most efficient work of the sort that has been attained in this country, and the one that is the most free from the taint of political favoritism.

In conclusion, a personal word. You have no doubt received many letters from clergymen and others all over the country on this same subject. Some will contain expressions of disagreement and even abuse. Do not be afraid of what is written by those who are afraid of a change, by the rich and their toadies, or by those who are offended because you do not act upon their own pet peeve. The masses of the people are still with you and you are their hope. Go on in the path that you have set out for yourself and you will ever enjoy the admiration and gratitude of the American people.

> With all good wishes, I remain,
> Yours sincerely,
> Rabbi Simon Cohen
> 587 East 8th Street
> Brooklyn, NY
> October 27, 1935

Source: Letter, Rabbi Simon Cohen to Franklin D. Roosevelt, October 27, 1935. President's Personal File, Entry 21. Franklin D. Roosevelt Presidential Library and Museum.

IMPORTANT PEOPLE, PLACES, AND TERMS

Agricultural Adjustment Act (AAA)
New Deal program passed in 1933 that sought to boost farm prices by reducing production of key crops.

America First Committee
Influential isolationist group in the United States that argued against America's entry into World War II.

Antitrust
Laws and legislative measures concerned with regulating business to protect against monopolies.

Bank Holiday
Temporary bank closures used to protect banks from massive depositor withdrawals.

Banking Act of 1933
Also known as the Glass-Steagall Act, this law instituted major reforms designed to shore up banks and protect the savings of depositors.

Bennett, Hugh Hammond (1881-1960)
Chief of the Soil Conservation Service during the Great Depression.

Capitalism
Economic system based on private ownership of manufacturing, goods, and services, with limited regulation of business practices.

Civilian Conservation Corps (CCC)
New Deal agency founded in 1933 that put millions of young Americans to work on conservation and land development projects.

Commodities
Goods such as farm crops or minerals that can be traded or bought and sold.

Coolidge, Calvin (1872-1933)
30th president of the United States who served from 1923 to 1929.

Coughlin, Charles (1891-1979)
Catholic priest who became famous for his anti-Semitic views and opposition to the New Deal.

Credit Plans
Installment payment plans that allowed buyers to pay for products a little at a time over a period of several months or years instead of paying the full purchase price at one time.

Dole
Distribution by government agencies of money, food, clothing, and other items to poor or unemployed people.

Dust Bowl
Region of the country in the Great Plains that struggled with drought and dust storms during the 1930s.

Emergency Banking Relief Act
New Deal legislation passed in 1933 that gave the president new authority to oversee banking practices.

Fascism
System of government marked by a strong central authority or dictator, promotion of extreme feelings of nationalism, and suppression of people or groups who hold other views.

Federal Emergency Relief Administration (FERA)
New Deal agency that provided employment to an estimated 20 million Americans on public works projects from 1933 to 1935.

First Hundred Days
Term used for President Roosevelt's first wave of legislative and economic reforms after he was inaugurated in 1933.

Ford, Henry (1863-1947)
Automobile maker who ranked as one of the most famous U.S. businessmen of the twentieth century.

Foreclosure

The legal process by which an owner's right to property is terminated, usually because of failure to pay money borrowed by the owner from a bank or other lending institution.

Glass-Steagall Act

Also known as the Banking Act of 1933, this law instituted major reforms designed to shore up banks and protect the savings of depositors.

Hawley-Smoot Tariff Act

Legislation passed in 1930 to increase taxes on imported goods; the act was meant to help U.S. farmers and businesses, but instead it worsened economic conditions in the United States and around the world.

Hoover, Herbert (1874-1964)

31st president of the United States who served from 1929 to 1933.

Hooverville

Nickname given to homeless communities that sprouted across the United States during the early years of the Depression.

Hopkins, Harry L. (1890-1946)

Director of the Works Progress Administration, one of the most important agencies of the New Deal era.

Ickes, Harold (1874-1952)

Secretary of the Interior for all four terms of the Roosevelt administration.

Isolationist

Someone who believes in avoiding involvement in the political, economic, or military affairs of other nations.

Jim Crow

Discriminatory laws across the American South that reduced African-American civil rights in virtually every area of life from the nineteenth century through the 1960s.

Johnson, Hugh S. (1882-1942)

Director of the National Recovery Administration during the New Deal era.

Lewis, John L. (1880-1969)

Union leader who was instrumental in the founding of the Congress of Industrial Organizations in the mid-1930s.

Long, Huey (1893-1935)

Louisiana governor and senator who called for massive wealth redistribution and other radical changes in American society.

National Industrial Recovery Act (NIRA)

Controversial legislation passed in 1933 that was designed to spur economic recovery and obtain the cooperation of American industry for New Deal reforms; it was declared unconstitutional by the U.S. Supreme Court in 1935.

National Labor Relations Act (NLRA)

One of the most important labor laws in U.S. history, this 1935 act gave unions the right to organize and bargain with employers on behalf of members.

National Recovery Administration (NRA)

A short-lived (1933-1935) New Deal agency that focused on fostering economic recovery by suspending regulatory restrictions on business and increasing worker rights.

National Youth Administration (NYA)

New Deal program that provided part-time employment to students to help them pay for school and apprenticeships.

New Deal

Term used to refer to the wide range of programs and policies introduced by the Roosevelt administration to promote economic recovery and social reform during the Depression.

Perkins, Frances (1882-1965)

Secretary of Labor in the Roosevelt administration during the Great Depression.

Prohibition

Period of U.S. history from 1920-1933 in which the manufacture and sale of almost all alcoholic beverages was outlawed.

Public Works
Construction projects such as schools, hospitals, and highways that are financed by public funds and built for the benefit or use of the general public.

Public Works Administration (PWA)
New Deal agency that oversaw construction of major public works projects across the country from 1933 to 1939.

Roosevelt, Eleanor (1884-1962)
Wife of Franklin D. Roosevelt who served as First Lady throughout the Great Depression and World War II.

Roosevelt, Franklin D. (1882-1945)
32nd president of the United States who served from 1933 to 1945.

Rural Electrification Administration (REA)
New Deal agency that extended electricity to rural areas across the United States during and after the Great Depression.

Social Security Act
A major 1935 law providing for federal aid for elderly and other vulnerable members of American society.

Soil Conservation Service
New Deal agency that helped develop more sustainable farming practices in the Great Plains, the Deep South, and other regions of the country during the Depression years.

Tariff
A tax on imported goods.

Tennessee Valley Authority (TVA)
New Deal agency that carried out major flood control, electrification, irrigation, and other programs in the Tennessee Valley region during and after the Depression.

Townsend, Francis (1867-1960)
American physician whose "Townsend Plan" for old-age pensions drew millions of supporters in the early 1930s.

Wagner, Robert F. (1877-1953)

Democratic Senator from New York who wrote and helped secure passage of the National Labor Relations Act, also known as the Wagner Act.

Wallace, Henry (1888-1965)

Head of the Department of Agriculture during the Great Depression, and Vice President of the United States for most of World War II.

Works Progress Administration (WPA)

The greatest of the New Deal agencies that put unemployed Americans to work on major public construction projects during the Depression.

CHRONOLOGY

1929

March—Herbert Hoover succeeds fellow Republican Calvin Coolidge as president of the United States. *See p. 16.*

October—The Stock Market Crash of 1929 begins on October 21; it wipes out the savings of millions of Americans and shatters the U.S. economy over the course of the ensuing eight days. *See p. 18.*

1930

March—President Herbert Hoover assures Americans that the nation's economy is back on the upswing and fundamentally sound. *See p. 24.*

June—The disastrous Hawley-Smoot Act is passed, imposing steep tariffs on a wide range of imported goods and materials. *See p. 26.*

More than 1,300 banks close their doors across the United States. *See p. 27.*

1931

February—Food riots break out in several cities across the United States. *See p. 29.*

Unemployment and foreclosures on homes and businesses soar to record levels.

1932

January—The Reconstruction Finance Corporation is created to provide loans to banks, insurance companies, railroads, and other lending institutions. *See p. 27.*

March—Unemployed auto workers clash with police and company security forces at the Ford Motor Company's plant in River Rouge, Michigan. *See p. 30.*

May—The Bonus March of World War I veterans begins in Portland, Oregon; the march ultimately brings thousands of veterans to Washington, D.C., in a failed attempt to collect "bonus" pay for their military service. *See p. 37.*

June—The Revenue Act of 1932 is passed, raising tax rates on individuals and corporations alike. *See p. 37.*

November—Democratic nominee Franklin D. Roosevelt easily defeats Herbert Hoover to claim the presidency of the United States. *See p. 38.*

1933

January—Adolf Hitler is appointed chancellor of Germany.

March—Roosevelt is inaugurated and delivers his famous address in which he tells the American people that "the only thing we have to fear is fear itself." *See p. 42.*

March 4—Roosevelt's famous "First Hundred Days" of legislation begins. *See p. 45.*

March 6—Roosevelt institutes a four-day bank holiday to give the administration and Congress time to create a plan to save the failing banking industry. *See p. 43.*

March 9—Congress passes the Emergency Banking Relief Act. *See p. 43.*

March 12—Roosevelt gives the first of his "fireside chat" national radio broadcasts. *See p. 44.*

March 31—The Civilian Conservation Corps (CCC) is established with the passage of the Unemployment Relief Act. *See p. 53.*

May 12—The Agricultural Adjustment Act is passed. *See p. 46.*

May 12—The Federal Emergency Relief Administration (FERA) is created. *See p. 48.*

May 12—The Emergency Farm Mortgage Act is passed.

May 18—Roosevelt signs legislation creating the Tennessee Valley Authority (TVA). *See p. 46.*

June 16—Passage of the National Industrial Recovery Act (NIRA) paves the way for the establishment of the National Recovery Administration (NRA) and the Public Works Administration (PWA). *See p. 49.*

June 16—The Glass-Steagall Act, also known as the Banking Act of 1933, is signed by Roosevelt. *See p. 44.*

October—The Roosevelt administration establishes the Civil Works Administration (CWA).

December—Prohibition comes to an end in the United States.

1934

May—A three-day dust storm blows an estimated 350 million tons of topsoil from the Great Plains all the way to the Eastern seaboard.

June—Roosevelt signs the Taylor Grazing Act, which allows him to take up to 140 million acres of federal land out of the public domain and establish new grazing rules and districts. *See p. 71.*

August—The anti-New Deal American Liberty League is founded. *See p. 90.*

1935

April—Roosevelt signs legislation paving the way for the creation of the Works Progress Administration (WPA), the greatest public works/employment program of the New Deal. *See p. 78.*

April 14—The "Black Sunday" blizzard hits the Dust Bowl. *See p. 63.*

The Soil Conservation Service is established in the Department of Agriculture by the April 27 passage of the Soil Conservation Act. *See p. 71.*

May—The U.S. Supreme Court rules that the National Recovery Administration is unconstitutional. *See p. 86.*

The Rural Electrification Administration (REA) is founded. *See p. 88.*

June—The National Youth Administration (NYA) is established. *See p. 88.*

July—The National Labor Relations Act becomes law. *See p. 84.*

August—Roosevelt signs the Social Security Act. *See p. 82.*

The Wealth Tax Act, derided by critics as Roosevelt's "soak the rich" tax, is passed. *See p. 78.*

September—Louisiana politician Huey Long is assassinated. *See p. 78.*

November—The Committee for Industrial Organization (CIO) is founded; three years later it takes the name Congress of Industrial Organizations. *See p. 87.*

1936

January—The U.S. Supreme Court rules that the Agricultural Adjustment Administration (AAA) is unconstitutional.

February—The City of Los Angeles establishes "bum blockades" at the city limits to keep migrants out. *See p. 70.*

November—Roosevelt defeats Democratic candidate Alf Landon to win a second term as president. *See p. 90.*

1937

July—Congress formally rejects Roosevelt's plan to "pack" the Supreme Court with new justices of his choosing. *See p. 92.*

August—Gradual economic gains of the past few years abruptly halt and the United States begins its slide into what comes to be known as the "Roosevelt recession." *See p. 93.*

1939

The long drought conditions that afflicted much of the country finally come to an end, helping farmers make an economic recovery after years of hardship. *See p. 73.*

September—World War II begins when Germany invades Poland, leading Great Britain and France in turn to declare war on Germany. *See p. 96.*

1940

September—The America First Committee is founded. *See p. 96.*

November—Roosevelt wins a third term as president by defeating Wendell Willkie. *See p. 99.*

1941

December 8—One day after Japan staged a surprise bombing of the U.S. Naval Base at Pearl Harbor, the United States declares war on Japan. *See p. 102.*

December 11—Germany and the United States declare war against one another. *See p. 102.*

1941-1945

The American economy makes a full recovery from the depths of the Great Depression, driven by soaring demand for wartime materials. *See p. 103.*

1945

April 12—Roosevelt dies and Harry S. Truman is sworn in as president. *See p. 107.*

May 7—Germany surrenders, ending World War II in Europe. *See p. 107.*

August 14—Japan surrenders eight days after the United States drops an atomic bomb on the Japanese city of Hiroshima and five days after a U.S. airplane drops a second atomic bomb on Nagasaki. Japan's surrender brings World War II to a close. *See p. 107.*

SOURCES FOR FURTHER STUDY

Allen, Frederick Lewis. *Only Yesterday: An Informal History of the 1920s.* 1931. New York: Harper Perennial, 2000. This is a reprint of a book written in the early stages of the Depression by a top journalist of the era. Regarded as a classic of American history, it describes the Roaring Twenties and the Crash of 1929 in vivid color.

Cohen, Robert, ed. *Dear Mrs. Roosevelt: Letters from Children of the Great Depression.* Chapel Hill: University of North Carolina Press, 2002. This sampling of letters received by the First Lady during the Depression shows the deep impact that the Depression had on America's children.

Egan, Timothy. *The Worst Hard Time.* Boston: Houghton Mifflin, 2006. A bestseller, this book describes life on the Great Plains during the Dust Bowl for those farmers and storeowners that decided to stay and try to survive.

Franklin D. Roosevelt Presidential Library and Museum. Available online at www.fdrlibrary.marist.edu. This World Wide Web site provides online access to a large selection of public papers, audio and video materials, and photographs covering various aspects of the Roosevelt presidency.

Goodwin, Doris Kearns. *No Ordinary Time: Franklin and Eleanor Roosevelt: The Home Front.* New York: Simon & Schuster, 1994. A fascinating account of the Roosevelt marriage and its ups and downs by one of the country's most famous historians.

Leuchtenberg, William E. *The FDR Years: On Roosevelt and His Legacy.* New York: Columbia University Press, 1995. This work provides an excellent overview of Roosevelt's performance as president, his New Deal agenda, and the beliefs that led him to pursue his reform policies.

New Deal Network. Available online at www.newdeal.feri.org. This research and teaching resource is devoted to the public works and art projects of the New Deal. It includes a wide range of materials, from Dust Bowl oral histories to art works sponsored by the Works Progress Administration and other New Deal agencies.

Watkins, T.H. *The Hungry Years: A Narrative History of the Great Depression in America.* New York: Owl Books, 2000. This wide-ranging popular history discusses all major events of the Depression in a colorful, informative manner.

BIBLIOGRAPHY

Books

Allen, Frederick Lewis. *Only Yesterday: An Informal History of the 1920s.* 1931. New York: Harper Perennial, 2000.

Badger, Anthony J. *The New Deal: The Depression Years, 1933-1940.* Chicago: Ivan R. Dee, 2002.

Blum, John M. *V was for Victory: Politics and American Culture during World War II.* New York: Harcourt Brace, 1976.

Brands, H.W. *Traitor to His Class: The Privileged Life and Radical Presidency of Franklin Delano Roosevelt.* New York: Doubleday, 2008.

Collier, Peter. *The Roosevelts: An American Saga.* New York: Simon and Schuster, 1994.

Davis, Kenneth S. *FDR: The New Deal Years, 1933-1937.* New York: Random House, 1986.

Egan, Timothy. *The Worst Hard Time.* Boston: Houghton Mifflin, 2006.

Galbraith, John Kenneth. *The Great Crash, 1929.* Boston: Houghton Mifflin, 1959.

Garraty, John. *The Great Depression.* New York: Doubleday, 1987.

Goodwin, Doris Kearns. *No Ordinary Time: Franklin and Eleanor Roosevelt: The Home Front.* New York: Simon & Schuster, 1994.

Gregory, James, *American Exodus: The Dust Bowl Migration and Okie Culture in California.* New York: Oxford University Press, 1989.

Hunt, John G., ed. *The Essential Franklin D. Roosevelt.* New York: Gramercy Books, 1995.

Leuchtenberg, William E. *The FDR Years: On Roosevelt and His Legacy.* New York: Columbia University Press, 1995.

Parrish, Michael. *Anxious Decades: America in Prosperity and Depression.* New York: Norton, 1992.

Polenberg, Richard. *The Era of Franklin D. Roosevelt, 1933-1945.* Boston: Bedford/St. Martins, 2000.

Rauchway, Eric. *The Great Depression and the New Deal.* New York: Oxford University Press, 2008.

Sitkoff, Harvard. *A New Deal for Blacks: The Emergence of Civil Rights as a National Issue. Vol. 1: The Depression Years.* New York: Oxford University Press, 1978.

Svobida, Lawrence. *Farming the Dust Bowl: A First-Hand Account from Kansas.* Reprint. Originally published as *An Empire of Dust,* 1940. Lawrence: University Press of Kansas, 1986.

Taylor, Nick. *American-Made: The Enduring Legacy of the WPA: When FDR Put the Nation to Work.* New York: Bantam, 2008.

Turkel, Studs. *Hard Times: An Oral History of the Great Depression.* New York: Pantheon, 1971.

Watkins, T.H. *The Hungry Years: A Narrative History of the Great Depression in America.* New York: Owl Books, 2000.

Online

The Eleanor Roosevelt Papers Project, Available online at http://www.gwu.edu/~erpapers/ (accessed May 2008).

"Franklin D. Roosevelt: Fireside Chats." Available online at the American Presidency Project, http://www.presidency.ucsb.edu/fireside.php (accessed May 2008).

"A New Deal for the Arts." Available online at the National Archives and Records Administration, htttp://www.archives.gov/exhibits/new_deal_for_the_arts/index.html (accessed May 2008).

"Surviving the Dust Bowl." Available online at *The American Experience,* http::www.pbs.org/wgbh/amex/dustbowl/ (accessed May 2008).

"TVA: Electricity for All." Available online at the New Deal Network, http://www.newdeal.feri.org/tva/index.htm (accessed May 2008).

DVDs

American Experience: FDR. DVD. PBS, 2006.

American Experience: Surviving the Dust Bowl. DVD. PBS, 1998.

FDR: A Presidency Revealed. DVD. History Channel/A&E Home Video, 2005.

Life in the Thirties. DVD. Project Twenty/Shanachie, 2003.

PHOTO AND ILLUSTRATION CREDITS

Cover and Title Page: Photo by Dorothea Lange, FSA/OWI Photograph Collection, Prints & Photographs Division, Library of Congress, LC-fsa 8b29523.

Chapter One: AP Photo (p. 8); National Photo Company Collection, Prints & Photographs Division, Library of Congress, LC-USZ62-111329 (p. 10), LC-USZ62-68543 (p. 12); Underwood & Underwood, Prints & Photographs Division, Library of Congress, LC-USZ62-24155 (p. 16); Fox Photos/Getty Images (p. 19).

Chapter Two: Prints & Photographs Division, Library of Congress, LC-USZ62-101365 (p. 25), LC-USZ62-49591 (p. 32); The Tony Spina Collection, Walter P. Reuther Library, Wayne State (pp. 26, 30); Photo by Arthur Rothstein, FSA/OWI Photograph Collection, U.S. Office of War Information, Prints & Photographs Division, Library of Congress, LC-fsa-8a09237 (p. 28); AP Photo (p. 36); Courtesy of the Franklin D. Roosevelt Digital Archives (p. 38).

Chapter Three: Courtesy of the Franklin D. Roosevelt Digital Archives (pp. 42, 46, 55, 56); U.S. Bureau of Reclamation, Prints & Photographs Division, Library of Congress, LC-DIG-ppmsca-17402 (p. 50); Brown Brothers, Sterling, PA 18463 (p. 53).

Chapter Four: Courtesy of American Experience/WGBH Educational Foundation. Copyright © 1998. WGBH/Boston. (p. 61); Photo by Arthur Rothstein, FSA/OWI Photograph Collection, Prints & Photographs Division, Library of Congress, LC-DIG-ppmsc-00241 (p. 63); Photo courtesy of USDA National Resources Conservation Service (p. 64); Photo by Dorothea Lange, FSA/OWI Photograph Collection, Prints & Photographs Division, Library of Congress, LC-DIG-fsa-8b29516 (p. 67), LC-DIG-ppmsca-03054 (p. 69); Brown Brothers, Sterling, PA 18463 (p. 72).

Chapter Five: State Library of Louisiana (p. 77); Photo by Barbara Wright, FSA/OWI Photograph Collection, Prints & Photographs Division, Library of Congress, LC-USW3-038668-D (p. 79); Art by Emanuel DeColas, Work Projects Administration Poster Collection, Prints & Photographs Division, Library of Congress, LC-USZC2-5370 (p. 81); Courtesy of the Franklin D. Roosevelt Digital Archives (p. 83); The Tony Spina Collection, Walter P. Reuther Library, Wayne State (p. 85); National Photo Company Collection, Prints & Photographs Division, Library of Congress, LC-DIG-npcc-06203 (p. 87); Photo by Arthur Rothstein, FSA/OWI Photograph Collection, Prints & Photographs Division, Library of Congress, LC-DIG-fsa-8b28231 (p. 89).

INDEX

O

P-Q

R